Srīmad Bhagavad Gītā

Chapter XVIII

The Text in Devanāgarī
with Transliteration in Roman letters,
Word-for-Word meaning in Text order

with

Translation

and

Commentary

by

Swāmī Chinmayānanda

CENTRAL CHINMAYA MISSION, TRUST

Printed upto	1982 to 1988		13,000 copies
Revised Edition	Oct. 1998 to July.	1999	2,000 copies
Revised Edition	Dec. 2001 to July.	2009	8,000 copies
Reprint	December	2010	1,000 copies

Published by :
CENTRAL CHINMAYA MISSION TRUST
Sandeepany Sadhanalaya,
Saki Vihar Road,
Mumbai 400 072, India
Tel. : (91-22) 2857 2367 / 2857 5806
Fax : (91-22) 2857 3065
E-mail : ccmtpublications@chinmayamission.com
Website : www.chinmayamission.com

Distribution Centre in USA :
CHINMAYA MISSION WEST
Publications Division,
560 Bridgetown Pike,
Langhorne, PA 19053, USA.
Phone : (215) 396-0390
Fax : (215) 396-9710
Email : publications@chinmayamission.org
Website : www.chinmayapublications.org

Printed by :
PRIYA GRAPHICS
Unit No. J - 120, Ansa Industrial Estate,
Saki Vihar Road, Sakinaka, (Andheri)
Mumbai - 400 072. (India)
Tel. No. 6695 9935 / 4005 9936
Email: chinmayapriya@hotmail.com

Price : Rs : 80=00

ISBN: 978-81-7597-098-4

Preface to the Revised Edition

The closing chapter (eighteen) is a peroration of the beautiful discourse of the inspired Divine and, therefore, is a reiteration of almost all the salient ideas and a summary of the whole *Gītā*--The Scripture of Mankind.

Niṣkāma Karma i.e., Unselfish work is an all-pervasive doctrine of the *Gītā.* Seeing the Divine Will working through the well-of-all, the enlightened ones offer all the fruits of action as well as abandon the sense of agency to the Lord. Expecting fruits of action or remuneration for services is natural and unavoidable for a man in the world. By cultivating a special attitude towards work--as an offering to God--work is turned into worship.

In all ancient societies and even amongst the modern European races till industrial revolution, there was a stratification of society into four classes--priest, nobility, agriculturist and traders, and serfs. These four character types are universal all over the world. The four-fold class system i.e., the four *Varṇa-s* of *Brāhmaṇa, Kṣatriya, Vaiśya* and *Śūdra* based on character types i.e., predominance of *Sāttvik, Rājasik and Tāmasik* in the constitution of their body-mind-equipment, rather than the four hereditary castes, is a great doctrine of the social philosophy of ancient India. Unfortunately it is the most misunderstood and misinterpreted doctrine which is the root cause of social and political evil in the present day India.

Gītā speaks of three types of *Siddhi-s* i.e., types of perfection. *Siddhi,* in general, means "attainment of the end in view of an undertaking." *Svadharma* being the integral nature of man, he can not give it up; he would be compelled to undertake his *Svadharma* by force of his Nature. Though Arjuna expressed a desire to retire to forest to take up the life of a medicant, his inherent *Kṣatriya* character dragged him back into the great war.

One devoted to *Svadharma* gains purity of mind and powerful aspiration through the grace of God reaches an advanced stage of development through dedicated performance, simultaneously accompanied by intense meditation and worship.

The second is described as *Naiṣkarmya Siddhi* i.e., "Perfection of transcendence of work," which is essentially the abandonment of 'fruits of action' and the 'sense of agency.'

The third *Siddhi* is *Brahma-bhūyam* wherein an introvert and ascetic is living in solitude absorbed in meditation, having nothing to do with the outside world, or any other work. He is workless both mentally and physically. It is the same state referred to as *Brāhmī-sthiti* (II-72), *Sthita-prajña* (II-54) and *Brahma-bhūya* (XIV-26).

Bhakti and *Jñāna* considered the same; at their highest reaches, both perfect each other. Concluding the whole teaching of *Gītā* in Verse 63, the Lord, in a true democratic style of the *Hindu* Commandments as contained in *Taittirīya Upaniṣad,* giving remarkable freedom to *Arjuna* says: "do as you think as fit." *Arjuna* having regained his true original nature of a soldier desired a "Clear command." Therefore, the Lord in Verses 65-66, to satisfy his friend and disciple says "Fix your mind upon me, be devoted to Me, sacrifice to Me, bow down to Me...." and then "abandoning all *dharma-s* (of the body, mind and intellect), take refuge in Me alone, I will liberate thee from all sins; grieve not."

Madhusūdana Sarasvatī draws a very fine distinction in the three forms of surrender based on the maturity of *Sādhanā:*--

i) "I am His"--i.e., the wave belongs to the ocean and never the other way round.

ii) "He is mine"--i.e., the devotee's sense of 'myness' is so great that the Lord can never separate Himself from his devotee.

iii) "He is I"--is the highest stage of surrender where 'I' has disappeared in the 'He', and there is only 'He.'

The term *'Jñāna Yajña'*-- used for the first time in the *Gītā*--means "sacrifice of knowledge" is a mental form of sacrifice which is the highest form of adoration of the Lord. Identification of man with the perishable body-mind-equipment is the root cause of this delusion. Lord's instructions restore man to be the Immortal Spirit.

In this revised Edition, diacritical marks are used for Transliteration of *Samskṛta* words in the verses as well as commentary. Non-English words have been italicised. *Transliteration* as well as word meanings have been added to *Gītā Dhyāna Śloka-s* too. In the 'free translation' section where the entire text is italicised, to distinguish *Samskṛta* words, 'normal' fonts are used. In the 'word-for-word meaning' section, for the benefit of readers not knowing *Devanāgarī* transliteration of *Samskṛta* words is added. This will help readers to identify and pronounce the words correctly.

An "Alphabetical Index" in *Devanāgarī* showing the first line of Verses, "Glossary of Terms used," "*Gītā Dhyāna Ślokas,*" "Index to Topics," "Appellations of Arjuna" "Names of *Śrī Kṛṣṇa*" have been added to the volume containing Chapter-I of the present series. An Alphabetical Index of Verses in Roman Scripts, ignoring *Devanāgarī* alphabetical order, showing the beginning of first and second lines of verses having two lines, and of first and third lines of verses having four lines has been added to the volume containing Chapter XVIII. This will be helpful in locating quotation from the middle of verses. The *Gītā* (chapter-wise) has been printed afresh in the revised format.

To be true to the *Samskṛta* text in transliteration, we have used "*Brāhmaṇa*" for the first *Varṇa* instead of the commonly used word "*Brahmin.*" It need not be confused with the term "*Brahman*" of the *Vedāntin-s.*

To facilitate easy location of a particular verse, distinctive marking are given on the top of each page along with Chapter No. and Name of the Chapter.

A key to the transliteration and pronunciation has been added in the beginning of the book.

Publishers

Chapter XVIII

LIBERATION THROUGH RENUNCIATION

INTRODUCTION

The *Gītā* is a piece of art of strange beauty and it stands apart from everything else, in a class all by itself. It is liquid poetry, expounding solid philosophy. In the fluidity of its metre, it crystallises some of the rarest gems of moral and spiritual values. Its breezy discourses have a firm style. The fluidity of its eloquence falls like merciful rain upon every broken personality, making it whole by its magic touch. It is not a book of science, and yet, it is very scientific in its approach to the theme. It has not the airy nothingness of familiar philosophical discourses, and yet, all philosophies seem to meet within its ample stretch.

It is the duty of science to *describe* life; it is the purpose of philosophy to *explain* life. Science describes the natural structures and processes; philosophy attempts their explanations. Thus viewed, the *Bhagavad Gītā* is an enchanting immpossibility; it is at once a science and a philosophy, and yet, strangely enough, it is neither a scientific philosophy nor a philosophical science. In its eighteen chapters, it explains a Philosophy of Living, and while doing so it also expounds and demonstrates the Science of Living.

When such a perfect combination of both science and philosophy is sung to the melody of perfection that *Kṛṣṇa* was, we have in this piece of work an appeal both to the head and the heart. This is, perhaps, the secret charm of the Lord's Song* that had enthralled generations from the day of its production some three thousand years before Christ.

This closing chapter of the *Gītā* is, in fact, a summary of the entire Song of the Lord. If the second chapter, as we found earlier, is a summary of the *Gītā* in anticipation, the eighteenth chapter is a report on the *Gītā* in retrospect.** It is already proved that, everywhere, the One Eternal Spirit functions through *matter,* and comes to express Itself in this pluralistic world of phenomena. The multiple world of plurality is extremely variegated in the nature, behaviour and quality of the individuals; variations in thousands of shades are noticed.

It was explained exhaustively-and in almost all the chapters there was some mention of this-that the distinctions depend upon the temperaments that predominate in each one's personality composition. On the basis of temperaments, the *Gītā* indicated three types of personalities: The "Good" *(Sāttvik),* the "Passionate" *(Rājasik)* and the "Dull" *(Tāmasik).* In this chapter we have an elaborate and exhaustive discussion on how these three temperaments, in their variations, create differences among individuals, in sacrifice, in wisdom, in actions, in fortitude and in happiness.

---

* *Bhagavad Gītā*

** Serious students who had been so far following these discourses very carefully, would do well now to go back to the beginning of the text and read the "introduction" given at the opening of each of the preceding seventeen chapters.

Also in the *Gītā* two familiar terms, "renunciation" (Sannyāsa) and "abandonment" *(Tyāga)* were very often used in different contexts with seemingly different imports. The terms have to be re-defined in order to remove all confusions, as an ambiguity in a science is dangerous to true understanding.

This chapter opens with a direct question from Arjuna as to what constitutes "renunciation" and what the contents of "abandonment" are. Lord *Kṛṣṇa* takes up the theme and starts defining these two terms; but some students of *Gītā* complain, "the *Gītācārya* has drifted away into a rambling discourse on various other topics unconnected with the main question." In fact, this is no fair criticism, Having defined what is *Sannyāsa,* the Lord explains Tyāga and shows how, through the latter alone, the former can be achieved and fully lived.

Unless we discover in ourselves the capacity to banish from our mind its various unhealthy relationships with the world outside and re-educate it to be continuously vigilant and alert to live in a healthy, intelligent spirit of detachment (*Tyāga),* the total withering away of the false ego and its endless desire-promptings, *Sannyāsa* can never be achieved. Abandonment is the true content of the status of renunciation; *Sannyāsa* without *Tyāga*-spirit is but an empty show; it is a false crown with no kingdom of joy within for it to lord over.

The endless, minute details given here, all true-to-life, analysing and classifying the tendencies, urges, emotions, actions etc., are pointers that help each one to understand himself. They are so many "instruments" on the "dash-board" of our bosom within, which can, by their indications, give us a true picture of the condition of the personality-mechanism working within us. Just as a driver of a car can understand the condition of the engine and the nature of its performance by watching the play of the "pointers" in the metres on the dash-board in front of him-heat, pressure, oil, charge, speed, fuel, mileage, ignition and what not-a seeker is asked to check up at similar definite "pointers" within and note their readings. If all are indicating the safe-sign, *Sāttvik,* a smooth life of maximum efficiency and definite progress in cultural evolution is promised. If we can classify ourselves in our tendencies and actions only as *Rājasik,* we are advised to take note and be cautious. If the tendencies declare a definite *Tāmasik* temperament, better halt the vehicle and attend to the "engine." This seems to be the advice of this concluding chapter.

The giving up of these lower impulses of the "Passionate" *(Rājasik)* and the Dull *(Tāmasik)* in our moment-to-moment contacts with life, is "abandonment" *(Tyāga),* which will give us sufficient mastery over ourselves, ultimately to give up the very ego-centre which causes all these defections. And this final giving up of the perception of the finite in the acquired wisdom of the Infinite is the fulfilment of life, indicated here by the term "Renunciation" *(Sannyāsa).*

ॐ

श्री परमात्मने नमः

अथ अष्टादशोऽध्यायः

अर्जुन उवाच-

संन्यासस्य महाबाहो तत्त्वमिच्छामि वेदितुम्।
त्यागस्य च हृषीकेश पृथक्केशिनिषूदन ।।१।।

Arjuna uvāca-
Sannyāsasya mahābāho tattvam-icchāmi veditum,
tyāgasya ca hṛṣīkeśa pṛthak-keśi-niṣūdana.

संन्यासस्य *sannyāsasya* = of renunciation; महाबाहो *mahābāho* = O mighty-armed; तत्त्वम् tattvam = the essence of truth; इच्छामि *icchāmi* = (I) wish; वेदितुम् veditum = to know; त्यागस्य *tyāgasya* = of *tyāga* or abandonment; ca = and; हृषीकेश *hṛṣīkeśa* = O *Hṛṣīkeśa,* पृथक् *pṛthak* = severally; केशिनिषूदन *keśi-niṣūdana* = slayer of *keśi.*

Arjuna Said :

1. *I desire to know severally, O mighty-armed, the essence or truth of 'Renunciation,' O Hṛṣīkeśa, as also of 'Abandonment,' O slayer of Keśi (Kṛṣṇa).*

The chapter begins with Arjuna's question, demanding of Lord Kṛṣṇa a precise definition, and an exhaustive explanation, of the two terms used by the Lord in the *Gītā*, off and on, here and there. 'Renunciation' *(Sannyāsa)* and 'Abandonment' *(Tyāga)* are the two technical terms used more than once in the *Gītā.* Though the question is asked in a spirit of academic interest, *Kṛṣṇa* takes up the question in all seriousness. When a disciple expresses his doubt, he invariably fails to express his exact difficulty. However, it is the duty of the teacher to discover the difficulty of the student and clear his doubt, as even the Lord of the *Gītā* does here.

The logic of the entire chapter revolves around the meanings of 'Renunciation' and 'Abandonment.' *Sannyāsa* without the spirit of *Tyāga* is incomprehensible, and if at all it is ever so practised, it can only be a sham pose. The bulk of the chapter maps out the tendencies, urges, impulses and motives that are to be abandoned, so that true 'Abandonment' of the undivine personality can effectively take place. We must read the chapter in this spirit, or else it will surely fail to influence us.

Slayer of Keśi *(Keśi-niṣūdana):-Keśi* was a *Daitya* who attacked *Kṛṣṇa* in the form of a horse. *Kṛṣṇa* killed him by tearing him into two halves.

Defining these terms and indicating the entire significance of their connotations, Kṛṣṇa says:

श्रीभगवानुवाच-
काम्यानां कर्मणां न्यासं संन्यासं कवयो विदुः।
सर्वकर्मफलत्यागं प्राहुस्त्यागं विचक्षणाः।।२।।

Śrī Bhagavān uvāca-
Kāmyānāṁ karmaṇāṁ nyāsaṁ
sannyāsaṁ kavayo viduḥ,
sarva-karma-phala-tyāgaṁ
prāhus-tyāgaṁ vicakṣaṇāḥ.

काम्यानाम् *kāmyānām* = (of) desireful; कर्मणाम् *karmaṇām* = of actions; न्यासम् *nyāsam* = the renunciation; संन्यासम् *sannyāsam* = renunciation; कवयः *kavayaḥ.* = the sages; विदुः

viduḥ. = understand; सर्व कर्म फल त्यागम् *sarva-karma-phala-tyāgam* = the abandonment of the fruits of all works; प्राहु: *prāhuḥ* = declare; त्यागम् *tyāgam* = abandonment; विचक्षणा: *vicakṣaṇāḥ* = the wise.

The Blessed Lord Said :

2. *The Sages understand* Sannyāsa *to be "the renunciation of work with desire"; the wise declare "the abandonment of the fruits of all actions" as Tyāga.*

"Totally giving up all desire-prompted activities" is renunciation, and abandonment is "giving up of all anxieties for enjoying the fruits-of-action." As they stand, both of them read almost the same to the uninitiated; for, all desires are always for the fruits of our actions. Thus, "renouncing desire-motivated activity" and "renouncing our anxiety for the fruit" would read the same for those who see only their superficial suggestions. No doubt, both mean giving up desire, but *Tyāga* is slightly different from *Sannāyāsa;* and yet, "abandonment" has an integral relationship with "renunciation." Action is an effort put forth in the present, which, in its own time, will, it is hoped, fulfil itself into the desired fruit. And, the fruit is what we reap later on as a result of the present action. A desireless action, therefore, belongs to the p*resent,* while the anxiety to enjoy the fruit (desire) is a disturbance of our mind regarding a *future* period of time. The fruit comes after the action; the fruit is the culmination of an action undertaken in the present.

Desire and agitation bring about restlessness, and the deeper the desire, the greater is the amount of dissipation of our energies within. A dissipated man cannot execute any piece of work with steady efficiency and true ardour. Also, it is to be noticed, desire is always ordered by the ego. Elimination of the ego is at once the sublimation of the individuality and the ascension of the individual from the lower realms of consciousness to the upper-most stratum of the effulgent universal Awareness, the One Eternal God.

The tragedy of life becomes complete if a desire-ridden individual comes under the endless persecution of steady anxiety to enjoy the fruits of his actions. Fruits-of-actions belong to the *future* and they are always ordered by the quality and quantity of the action in the present moment, and also by the circumstances available in the chosen field of activity. Naturally, without the "Abandonment" *(Tyāga)* of our clinging attachment to the expected *fruits of our actions,* we will not discover the full potentialities of our own personality. Without this, our activities can never provide for us enjoyable fruits.

In short, "Renunciation" is the goal to be reached through the process of "Abandonment" of our moment-to-moment anxiety to enjoy the fruits. "Abandonment" *(Tyāga)* is the means to reach the goal of "Renunciation" *(Sannyāsa).*

Both *Sannyāsa* and *Tyāga* are disciplines in our activities. *Kṛṣṇa* is never tired of emphasising the importance of work. Neither of these terms indicates that work should be ignored; on the other hand both of them insist that work we must. Work, however, can gain a total transmutation by the removal of the things that clog our efficiency, and thus every piece of work can be made to yield its fullest reward. Snapping the chains that shackle us with the past and the future, and working without being hustled by anxieties or henpecked by desires, in the full freedom and inspiration of the present, is the noblest way to perform actions. To a large extent, we can say that the definition of these two terms in the *Gītā* is more broad-minded and tolerant than the implications of these two words as we read in the *Vedik lore.*

Should the ignorant perform work or not ?

त्याज्यं दोषवदित्येके कर्म प्राहुर्मनीषिण: ।
यज्ञदानतप:कर्म न त्याज्यमिति चापरे ।। ३ ।।

Tyājyaṁ doṣa-vadityeke karma prāhur-manīṣiṇaḥ
yajña-dāna-tapaḥ-karma na tyājyam-iti cāpare.

त्याज्यम् *tyājyam* = should be abandoned: दोषवत् *doṣavat* = (full of) as an evil इति *iti* = thus; एके *eke* = some; कर्म *karma* = actions; प्राहु: *prāhuḥ* = declare; मनीषिण: *manīṣiṇaḥ* = philosophers; यज्ञ-दान-तप:-कर्म *yajña-dāna-tapaḥ-karma* = acts of sacrifice, charity, and austerity; न *na* not; त्याज्यम् *tyājyam* = should be relinquished; इति *iti = thus* च *ca* = and; अपरे *apare* = others.

3. That all actions should be abandoned as evil, declare some philosophers; while others (declare) that acts of sacrifice, gift and austerity should not be relinquished.

In the previous stanza it was conclusively declared that *abandonment* is the "way" and total *renunciation* is the "goal." On this theory of abandonment, there is a school of philosophers, the *Sāṅkhya-s,* who declare: *"Action should be abandoned as an evil."* According to them, all actions are productive of *vāsanā-s* which cloud the realisation of the Self; and therefore, without exception, all actions should be renounced. Some commentators upon the *Sāṅkhyan* philosophy point out that *"work is not to be abandoned, except when it is going in wrong channels, motivated by demoniac urges like passion, greed, desire etc."*

The philosophers not only indicate that all seekers should avoid unhealthy activities which have, in their reactions, a deadening influence upon the spiritual beauty in man, but also advise that every man should engage himself in creative, character-moulding, moral-rebuilding work that can aid the individual's personality-integration. This latter school of thinkers recommend that 'sacrifice' *(Yajña),* 'charity' *(Dāna)* and 'austerity' (Tapas) should never be abandoned.

Śrī Saṅkarācārya, however, wants to read his pet doctrine in these lines, and almost with a reckless daring tries to twist and squeeze the stanza to bring his particular meaning out of it. *Śaṅkara* says that this is applicable only to those who practise the 'Yoga of Action' *(Karma-Yoga),* while for those who have reached the stage of knowledge *(Jñānī)* "complete abandonment of all work is imperative." This twist is considered as unnatural and unnecessary by many of his critics. As students of the *Gītā,* we should know that *Kṛṣṇa* wants Arjuna only to renounce all evil activities, and perform worldly work in a spirit of dedicated, selfless devotion; *Kṛṣṇa's Gītā,* calls upon man to make work itself the greatest homage unto the Supreme;

this is the spiritual *sādhanā* .

The Lord's decree is that the ignorant should perform work. Now, as to these divergent views:

निश्चयं श्रृणु मे तत्र त्यागे भरतसत्तम।
त्यागो हि पुरुषव्याघ्र त्रिविधः संप्रकीर्तितः।। ४।।

Niścayaṁ śṛṇu me tatra tyage bharata-sattama,
tyāgo hi puruṣa-vyāghra trividhaḥ saṁpra-kīrtitaḥ

निश्चयम् *niścayaṁ* = conclusion or the final truth; श्रृणु *śṛṇu* = hear; मे me = my; तत्र *tatra* = there; त्यागे *tyāge* = about abandonment; भरतसत्तम *bharatasattama* = O best of the *Bhārata-s;* त्यागः *tyāgaḥ* = abandonment हि *hi* = verily; पुरुष-व्याघ्र *puruṣa-vyāghra* = O best of men; त्रिविधः *trividhaḥ* = of three kinds; संप्रकीर्तितः *saṁprakīrtitaḥ* = has been declared (to be).

4. *Hear from me the conclusion or the final truth, about this "abandonment", O best of the* Bhārata-s; *"abandonment," verily, O best of men, has been declared to be of three kinds.*

Lord *Kṛṣṇa* is now promising Arjuna that he will scientifically explain what constitutes *Tyāga* and under what headings this spirit of 'abandonment' can be considered.

The discussion here is not mere indulgent literary curiosity, but is a definite technique to be practised and followed. For a mortal mind, giving up is no easy task; acquisition and aggrandisement are the very life-breath of man's mind. Naturally therefore, *Kṛṣṇa* has to invoke the best in *Arjuna* by addressing him as the "best among *Bhārata-s" (Bharata-Sattama)* and as a "tiger among men" *(Puruṣa-Vyāghra).*

"Abandonment" *(Tyāga)* for purposes of study and understanding, is three-fold. All through the *Gītā* this three fold classification is followed, and everywhere we find that it is classed as the 'pure' *(Sāttvik),* the 'passionate' *(Rājasik)* and the 'dull' *(Tāmasik).* However, *Śrī Rāmānuja* divides 'abandonment' into:

(1) abandonment of fruit;
(2) abandonment of the idea that the Self is an agent and, therefore, giving up all attachments; and
(3) abandonment of the 'actor-senses' in the realisation that Lord is the author of all actions.

This again is an example of how *Achāryā-s,* wedded to their pet doctrine, squeeze out their own meanings, with the result that the smooth stanzas get bulged out of all proportions of beauty to become positively ugly.

What is the decree then? *The Lord says:*

यज्ञदानतप:कर्म न त्याज्यं कार्यमेव तत् ।
यज्ञो दानं तपश्चैव पावनानि मनीषिणाम् ।। ५ ।।

Yajña-dāna-tapaḥ-karma na tyājyaṁ kāryameva tat,
yajño dānaṁ tapaś-caiva pāvanāni manīṣiṇām

यज्ञ-दान-तप:-कर्म *yajña-dāna-tapaḥ-karma* = acts of sacrifice, charity and austerity; न *na* = not; त्याज्यम् *tyājyam* = should be abandoned; कार्यम् *karyam* = should be performed; एव *eva* = indeed; तत् *tat* = that; यज्ञ: *yajñaḥ* = (worship) sacrifice; दानम् *dānam* = charity, gift; तप: *tapaḥ* = austerity; च *ca* = and; एव *eva* = indeed; पावनानि *pāvanāni* = purifies; मनीषिणाम् *manīṣiṇām* = of the wise.

5. *Acts of sacrifice, charity and austerity should not be abandoned, but should be performed; worship, charity,*

and also austerity, are the purifiers of even the 'wise.'

What has been said earlier has been accepted and emphasised. Practice of worship *(Yajña),* charity *(Dāna),* and austerity *(Tapas)* should not be abandoned. We have already found, in the previous chapter that these, when properly pursued, bring about a brilliant discipline within and create conditions under which alone, the highest spiritual unfoldment and the final experience of the Infinite are possible. *Kṛṣṇa* says here that these can "purify even thoughtful men." Men of evolutionary tendencies, who seek freedom from their personality-obsessions must, with devotion and the right attitude of mind, perform *Yajña-s, Dāna* and *Tapas.* Thereby they can discover an endless amount of inner peace and balance.

Obligatory work should be performed without attachment:

एतान्यपि तु कर्माणि सङ्गं त्यक्त्वा फलानि च ।
कर्तव्यानीति मे पार्थ निश्चितं मतमुत्तमम् ।।६।।

Etānyapi tu karmāṇi saṅgaṁ tyaktvā phalāni ca,
Kartavyānīti me pārtha niścitaṁ matam-uttamam

एतानि *etāni* = these, अपि *api* = even; तु *tu* = but; कर्माणि *karmāṇi* = actions; सङ्गम् *saṅgam* = attachment; त्यक्त्वा *tyaktvā* = leaving; फलानि *phalāni* = fruits; च *ca* = and; कर्तव्यानि *kartavyāni* = should be performed; इति *iti* = thus; मे *me* = my; पार्थ *pārtha* = *O Pārtha;* निश्चितम् *niścitam* = certain; मतम् *matam* = belief; उत्तमम् *uttamam* = best

6. *But even these actions should be performed leaving aside attachment and the fruits,* O Pārtha; *this is my*

certain and best belief.

Even these actions, namely, 'Sacrifice' *(Yajña),* 'Charity' *(Dāna)* and *(Tapas)* should be performed *"leaving attachments and fruits."* The term "attachment" in the *Gītā* has a peculiar flavour, and throughout, this term has been used to indicate the spirit in which an ego-centric personality will come to work in any field of activity, while fulfilling its own ego-centric desires. Thus, an ego and its desires are the component parts of attachments. When an ego strives to fulfil its own burning desires, it comes to live in a certain relationship with the world of things and objects around-this wrong relationship is called *"attachment."*

Once an individual starts working under the poison of "attachment," he comes to entertain an unintelligent, self-destructive anxiety to gain and enjoy the results of his actions. Long before the actions are completed, one's hope and hunger for their fruits can present themselves to weave a charm of their own, benumbing one's efficiency in the field of the action undertaken.

The idea that charity, sacrifice and austerity must be performed in an attitude of "detachment," "renouncing all anxieties for the enjoyment of the fruits" is, *Kṛṣṇa* admits, his own personal opinion *(matam).* It is not, however, purely an original *Kṛṣṇa*-creed, but is perfectly in line with the technique of selfless action as advised in all the *Hindū* scriptures. Most probably *Kṛṣṇa* is now confident that for Arjuna, the new convert, the Lord Himself is more authoritative than the old *Ṛṣi-s.* Therefore, to bless his devotee, *Kṛṣṇa* says that He is the author of this opinion.

To get rid of attachment and to be free from anxieties regarding the fruits that are yet to present themselves as a reward for the work undertaken in the present, are the main limbs of the *Kṛṣṇa*-creed in the *Gītā.* To live this *Kṛṣṇa*-way-of-action is to assure for outselves a healthy inner equipment, which can tenderly guide us to the peaks of Super manhood. The loving term used here by *Kṛṣṇa* in addressing *Arjuna* has its own appeal to the Prince. It recommends to him the *Kṛṣṇa*-theory of "abandonment" *(Tyāga),* as explained in this stanza.

Therefore, for a seeker of spiritual liberation, work is unavoidable; and with a proper spirit of tyāga, work can help him on his path. The Tāmasik tyāga' is:

नियतस्य तु संन्यासः कर्मणो नोपपद्यते ।
मोहात्तस्य परित्यागस्तामसः परिकीर्तितः ।। ७ ।।

Niyatasya tu sannayāsaḥ karmaṇo nopapadyate,
mohāt-tasya parityāgas-tāmasaḥ parikīrtitaḥ.

नियतस्य *niyatasya* = obligatory; तु *tu* = verily; संन्यासः *saṁnyāsaḥ* = renunciation; कर्मणः *karamaṇaḥ* = of action; न *na* = not; उपपद्यते *upapadyate* = is proper; मोहात् *mohāt* = from delusion; तस्य *tasya* = of the same; परित्यागः *parityāgaḥ* = abandonment; तामसः *tamāsaḥ* = *tāmasik;* परिकीर्तितः *parikīrtitaḥ* = is declared.

7. *Verily, the renunciation of "obligatory actions" is not proper; the abandonment of the same from delusion is declared to be Tāmasik (dull).*

Abandonment of obligatory duties is considered by the Lord as the lowest and the darkest. Every individual has his own obligations to himself and to others in the society. They include both the unavoidable *daily duties,* as well as the *special duties* that arise on special occasions in the life of an individual, and in the society of the times. Therefore, as long as an individual is a member of the society, enjoying the social life, and demanding protection and profit from the society, he has no right, according to the *Hindu* code-of-living, to abandon his "obligatory actions."

Even if one abandons one's moral duties in ignorance, one is not excused; for, as in the civil laws of the modern world and in the physical laws of the phenomenal world, so in the spiritual kindgom also, "ignorance of the law is no excuse." Out of ignorance and lack of proper thinking, if an individual ignores his obligations and refuses to serve the world he is living in, that 'abandonment' is considered as 'dull' *(Tāmasik).*

***The Rājasik tyāga* is:**

दु:खमित्येव यत्कर्म कायक्लेशभयात्त्यजेत् ।
स कृत्वा राजसं त्यागं नैव त्यागफलं लभेत् ।। ८ ।।

Duḥkham-ityeva yat-karma kāya-kleśa-bhayāt-tyajet,
sa kṛtvā rājasaṁ tyāgaṁ naiva tyāga-phalaṁ labhet.

दु:खम् *duḥkham* = (it is) painful; इति *iti* = thus; एव *eva* = even; यत् *yat* = which; कर्म *karma* = action; काय-क्लेश-भयात् *kāya-kleśa-bhayāt* = from fear of bodily trouble; त्यजेत् *tyajet* = abandons; स: *saḥ* - he; कृत्वा *kṛtva* = performing; राजसम् *rājasam* = *rājasik;* त्यागम् *tyāgam* = abandonment; न *na* = not; एव *eva* = even; त्याग-फलम् *tyāga-phalam* = the fruit of abandonment; लभेत् *labhet* = obtains.

8. He who, from fear of bodily trouble, abandons action because it is painful, thus performing a Rājasik (passionate) abandonment. obtains not the fruit of "abandonment."

Someone may come to give up his individual obligatory duties *"because they are painful"* or *"through fear of bodily suffering."* The *'relinquishment' or abondonment thus* practised falls under the "passionate" type *(Rājasik).* This clearly shows in its unsaid suggestions that a man of action and passion *(Rajas)* will readily undertake to act and fulfil his obligatory duties if they are not painful, and are not too fatiguing. To become a man of action, fulfilling all obligations and performing all duties without sacrificing one's own personal comforts, is no heroic life at all. Such actions have no special reward. In fact, *Kṛṣṇa* says : *"He shall attain no fruit whatsoever of his abandonment."*

Performance of one's obligatory duties is itself the most glorious of all forms of *"Tyāga,"* and it can be considered doubly so, when it involves a certain amount of sacrifice of one's own personal convenience and bodily comfort. *Arjuna* himself was hesitating to fight the battle which was his obligatory duty. *Arjuna's* 'relinquishment' of this duty could be considered as falling under this category of *Rājasik Tyāga.*

Real abandonment should always lead us on to the ampler fields of self-expression, push us into the fuller ways of living, and introduce us to the greater experiences of joy. A bud *abandons* itself to become a flower, the flower gives up its soft petals and its enchanting fragrance and gains for itself the richer status of a fruit. Every real abandonment should haul us up into a nobler status of fulfilment.

What then is the Sāttvik abandonment ?

कार्यमित्येव यत्कर्म नियतं क्रियतेऽर्जुन ।

सङ्गं त्यक्त्वा फलं चैव स त्यागः सात्त्विको मतः ॥९॥

Kāryam-ityeva yat-karma niyataṁ kriyate-'rjuna.

saṅgaṁ tyaktvā phalaṁ caiva sa tyāgaḥ sāttviko mataḥ

कार्यम् *kāryaṁ* = ought to be done; इति *iti* = thus; एव *eva* = even; यत् *yat* = which; कर्म *karma* = action; नियतम् *niyatam* = obligatory; क्रियते *kriyate* = is performed; अर्जुन *Arjuna* = *O Arjuna;* सङ्गम् *saṅgam* = attachment; त्यक्त्वा *tyaktvā* = abandoning; फलम् *phalam* = fruits; च *ca* = and; एव *eva* = even; सः *saḥ* = that; त्यागः *tyāgaḥ* = abandonment; सात्त्विकः *sāttvikaḥ* = *sāttvik* (pure); मतः *mataḥ* = is regarded.

9. *Whatever "obligatory action" is done, O Arjuna merely because it ought to be done, abandoning "attachment and also fruit," that abandonment is regarded as Sāttvik (pure).*

Those who execute thoroughly all their obligatory duties "because they are to be done" *(kāryam iti),* because to remain without accomplishing them is almost death to them-fall under the *Sāttvik* (pure) variety. They believe that certain acts of 'relinquishment' must be done, for otherwise, according to them, it is just insufferably indecent. When such persons, under these inspiring ideas, come to serve the community, or work in any field, they provide us with examples of the *Sāttvik* type of 'relinquishment.'

Activities have certain unavoidable encumbrances. All that the Lord says in the *Gītā* amounts only to this; that we must act on without these encumbrances curtailing and limiting our freedom of action. Thus, the *tyāga* of the good *(Sāttvik),* or real *tyāga,* means doing actions with the correct mental attitude." This may seem strange, but those who have carefully gone through these three stanzas explaining the true type of *tyāga* must have understood that all these discussions were not so much on what is to be 'relinquished' but as to *how* we must 'abandon,' and in which field we must act. In short, Lord *Kṛṣṇa's* concept of *Tyāga* condemns abandonment of the world and our duties in it. To the Lord in the *Gītā, Tyāga* is a subjective renunciation of all inner selfishness and desire, which limit the freedom of the individual in his field-of-activity. It is something like the abandonment that everyone practises in his dining room; renunciation of hunger by positively taking the food!

These are the sensitive touches that raise the status of the *Gītā,* as a philosophical art-piece which has at many points improved upon the philosophy of the *Upaniṣad-s* as was then understood by the *Arjuna*-generation. Not that the *Gītā,* has contributed any new theory or creed, but in its outright, matter-of-fact, down-to-the-earth practical discussions it has made the old ideas of the *Upaniṣad-s* relive, groomed and re-dressed to suit the fashion of thought in the modern times.

In these three stanzas the abandonment *(Tyāga)* discussed is not "the Abandonment of actions" but "abandonment of such things within our subjective personality that block the free flow of our own possibilities."

Tyāga makes an active man a more potential worker in the world.

Acting in the world outside, renouncing both the ego and the ego-centric desires, an individual comes to exhaust his *vāsanā-s,* and grows in his inward purity.

How does such a pure man, purified through Sāttvik Tyāga come to gain the highest spiritual experience?

न द्वेष्ट्यकुशलं कर्म कुशले नानुषज्जते ।
त्यागी सत्त्वसमाविष्टो मेधावी छिन्नसंशयः ।। १० ।।

Na dveṣṭya-kuśalaṁ karma kuśale nānu-ṣajjate,
tyāgī sattva-samā-viṣto medhāvī chinna-saṁśayaḥ.

न *na* = not; द्वेष्टि *dveṣti* = hates; अकुशलम् *akuśalam* = disagreeable; कर्म *karma* = actions; कुशले *kuśale* = to an agreeable one; न *na* = not; अनुषज्जते *anuṣajjate* = is attached; त्यागी *tyāgī* = the abandoner; सत्त्व-समाविष्टः *sattva samāviṣṭaḥ* = pervaded by purity; मेधावी *medhāvī* = intelligent; छिन्न-संशयः *chinna-saṁśayaḥ* = with his doubts cut asunder.

10. The abandoner, soaked in purity, being intelligent, with all his doubts cut asunder, hates not disagreeable action, nor is he attached to an agreeable action.

The previous stanza would, at the outset, look as an impossible thesis to any strong man of action and adventure. Perhaps the royal heart of *Arjuna* could not comprehend such a person who fulfils his obligatory duty "only because it ought to be done: *(kāryam iti)* renouncing attachment and fruit." As though answering the look of surpise on *Arjuna's* face, which faithfully registers his failure to appreciate the idea, *Kṛṣṇa* gives in this stanza a more elaborate picutre of such an individual.

A man established in *Sāttvik* abandonment never hates, nor does he ever feel attached. He is not miserable in disagreeable environment nor does he get attached to the circumstances and schemes-of-things which are aggreeable to his taste. He does his duties under all circumstances agreeable or disagreeable, without feeling elated when he finds himself on the "peaks" or feeling dejected when he discovers himself in the "pits" of life.

He is overwhelmed neither by extreme joy, nor by extreme sorrow; equanimity becomes his essential nature. He stands as a rock, ever at ease, and watches with an unbroken balance-of-vision, the waves of happenings rising and falling all around him, at all times. He is, in short, independent of the happenings in the outer world around him.

When, to such a man *of Sāttvik Tyāga,* impulses such as jealousy, anger, passion, greed etc. come, he does not get involved in these impulses, as we do in our attachments and identifications with them. That is, a man of abandonment *(tyāga)* readily discovers in himself a secret faculty to abandon his identification with the false, the lower instincts in himself. He does not become a victim of his own mental impressions *(vāsanā-s);* he stands ever free and surely apart from the tumults of his mind.

Such a man is said to be an educated and cultured man. An uncultured man is like a dry leaf that is tossed hither and thither by every passing breeze; such a person is like a reed upon the bosom of the sea, rising and falling in the mad revelry of the tireless waves. It is the privilege of the animal alone to get faithfully coloured by its own instincts and act according to the dictates of its impulses. It is only man, the inheritor of an intellect, who can enquire into the nature of the rising waves of impulses, judge them in the light of the ideal he holds onto in himself, and, if need be, stand apart from them and allow them to die away.

But ordinarily, an individual finds it impossible to stand apart and live, to act independently of his impulses. according to the *Gītā.* this is because man has allowed his faculty of 'abandonment' *Tyāga* to die away. A *Tyagī* is he who has cultivated this habit to live intellgently in life practising from moment to moment the 'abandonment' of all the animal whisperings in himself, and following diligently the Melody of the Soul. Such a man is established in *Sāttvik Tyāga.*

In order that one may come to judge correctly and renounce the false, one must have a very clear and steady picture of the Perfect in oneself. *Medhā-śakti* is not merely the intellect's power of understanding or reasoning, but it is also the intellect's *faculty to memorise and retain things.* A cultured man of unbroken equipoise and steady understanding must have a constant memory of :

(1) the constituents of the field of his activity;
(2) the instruments through which he contacts the world outside:
(3) his own essential infinitely divine nature; and
(4) his exact relationship with the world-of-objects when he is contacting it through his senses.

Such a person is called *Medhāvī, "a man of firm understanding."* And in case his knowledge be spotted with patches of doubts or slightly poisoned by traces of false knowledge, there will be in him endless confusions, which in their turn will bring about wrong judgements. Therefore, *Kṛṣṇa* indicates that a man of *Sāttvik Tyāga* is one whose *"doubt is cleft."*

The highest type of *Tyāga* is not, perhaps, abundantly found except in a minority who have accomplished their detachments from all their matter-vestures completely. But to the majority, identification with the body-mind-intellect equipment is so natural that they have the sense of agency and come to live in the world, conditioned by the happenings around. Such an average man, who works with an ego and attachment, must learn to work, at least renouncing the fruit.

Kṛṣṇa explains:

न हि देहभृता शक्यं त्यक्तुं कर्माण्यशेषतः।
यस्तु कर्मफलत्यागी स त्यागीत्यभिधीयते ।। ११।।

Na hi dehabhṛtā śakyaṁ tyaktuṁ karmāṇya-śeṣataḥ,
yastu karma-phala-tyāgī sa tyagī -tyabhi-dhīyate.

न *na* = not; हि *hi* = verily; देहभृता *dehabhṛtā* = by an embodied being; शक्यम् *śakyam* - possible; त्यक्तुम् tyaktym = to abandon; कर्माणि *karmāṇi* = actions; अशेषतः *aśeṣataḥ* = entirely; यः *yaḥ* = who; तु *tu* = but; कर्म-फल-त्यागी *karma-phala-tyāgī* = relinquisher of the fruits of actions; सः *saḥ* = he; त्यागी *tyāgī* = relinquisher; इति iti = thus; अभिधीयते *abhidhīyate* = is called.

11. *Verily, it is not possible for an embodied being to abandon actions entirely, but he who relinquishes "the fruits of actions" is verily called a 'relinquisher' (Tyāgī).*

To the rough-and-ready intellect in Arjuna, the easier method seems to be to escape all chances of action at once and thus in one sweep, renouncing altogether the contentious world, run to the jungle and live there in equanimity! The stanza now under review warns us against such a false conclusion. Actions we will have to perform. Without action no living organism can continue living. Existence itself is the manifestation of life's activities. To remain without doing anything is itself an action, and the physiological and psychological actions continue upto the grave. Anything that has a body, even a unicellular organism, can never hope to abandon all activities. Actions are the insignia of life. It is the fragrance in the flower-of-existence. Where there is no action, there life has ended; there existence has withered away-the substance has dried up... stinking death has come.

Since all of us are embodied, and therefore, cannot abandon all activities as long as we live, the only choice left to us is to direct and discipline all our actions in such a way as to bring a harmony into our inner life and a dynamic rhythm into our outer duties.

If *Tyāga* of the *Sāttvik* type is not possible for all of us, due to our attachments to the world-of-matter, certainly we can practise the 'abandonment' of at least our clinging attachments and anxieties for the fruits of our actions. Action cannot be completely abandoned by one who is conditioned by the gross, subtle and causal bodies. Such an individual-and most of us at this stage of our evolution fall under this category-is advised by *Kṛṣṇa to* abandon his anxiety to enjoy the fruits of his actions which are yet to come in a future period of time and act diligently, entirely, and enthusiastically in the present. A man who thus abandons the thirst to enjoy the fruits of his actions is called a *Tyāgī.*

Now what is the benefit which comes from Tyāga? *The Lord answers :*

अनिष्टमिष्टं मिश्रं च त्रिविधं कर्मणः फलम् ।
भवत्यत्यागिनां प्रेत्य न तु संन्यासिनां क्वचित् ।। १२।।

Aniṣṭa-miṣṭaṁ miśraṁ ca trividhaṁ karmaṇaḥ phalam,
bhavatya-tyāginām pretya na tu saṁnyāsinām kvacit.

अनिष्टम् *aniṣṭam* = unwise or disagreeable or evil; इष्टम् *iṣṭam* = desired or agreeable or good; मिश्रम् *miśram* = mixed; च *ca* = and; त्रिविधम् *trividham* = threefold; कर्मणः *karmaṇaḥ* = of action; फलम् *phalam* = fruit; भवति *bhavati* = accrues; अत्यागिनाम् *atyāginām* = to non-abandoners; प्रेत्य *pretya* = after death; न *na* = not; तु *tu* = but; संन्यासिनाम् *saṁnyāsinām* = to abandoners; क्वचित् *kvacit* = ever

12. *The threefold fruits of action-evil, good and mixed accrues, after death, only to those who have no spirit of 'abandonment'; never to total relinquishers.*

The results of all actions depend, it is said, upon the quality of the actions. Abandonment *(tyāga)* has already been described as belonging to three different categories. Here we have a discussion of the different types of reactions that would accrue when the different types of *tyāga* are practised.

Projection of a wilful desire in the world outside is an action, and according to the purity of the motive and the serenity of composure of the actor, a psychological reaction is left behind at the end of every activity. The mind has an instinctive habit of repeating itself. Future thoughts faithfully follow the foot-prints left by the past thoughts. Thus, actions in the world determine the "thought tendencies" of the human mind, and these tendencies *(vāsanā-s)* condition the mental equipment and order our reactions to the things that are happening around. The fruit-of-action, in philosophy, is not only its manifested results in the material world, but also the subtle constitutional changes it leaves in the thought-personality of man.

The total reactions gained by the mind's working in the world, according to Lord *Kṛṣṇa* fall under three distinct types:

(1) the disagreeable or the calamitous-meaning those that are positively bad;

(2) agreeable or non-calamitous-meaning positively good;

(3) the mixed type of balanced or average-wherein the tendencies are balanced equally between the good and the bad.

In the constant flow of time, the present determines the immediate future, and therefore, these tendencies, in their different textures, must necessarily determine our reactions to our environments in the immediate future. If we extend this theory to the very last moment of our days in this embodiment, it becomes amply evident that, after the departure from here through death, our next embodiment and the general type of environment that we will find ourselves in, would be determined by the type of tendencies produced by our actions. This is what is called the "reincarnation theory" in the *Sanātana Dharma.*

If the *vāsanā-s* are good *(Sāttvik),* then a joyous field of prosperity and happiness would be the only realm wherein such a mind would discover its destiny. Those who are entertaining and deliberately cultivating the low animal *vāsanā-s* in themselves will find for themselves a complete fulfilment only by appearing in the lower strata of life. When the 'tendencies' for good and bad are almost equal *(miśram),* then we enter into this world-of-action-the world in which we are now living-the world of the intelligent man. No doubt, in each of us there is a call of the "higher" constantly leading us towards an undetermined and indeterminable ideal, but there are also the barkings and the brayings, the hissings and the roars, of the "lower" in us, constantly confusing and systematically distracting our vision of the ideal.

If an individual were to identify himself with the higher and live up to the ideal as best as he can, the "higher" *vāsanā-s* will multiply and ultimately silence the "lower" completely. If, on the other hand, as is the fashion in the modern world, we allow ourselves to be tempted by the 'lower' and identify with the animal-impulses in us, they will multiply and make us a caricature of the Divine, that we really are. In short, in the tug-of-war between the 'higher' and the 'lower,' the determining factor is the individual's own personality.

In both these *vāsanā-s* grow, be they good or bad, and in either case, there is still a manifestation as birth in the realm of pangs and perils. The transcendence of the experiencer-personality is possible only when the conditionings have totally ended and the *vāsanā-s* are rendered powerless to hold the Pure Spirit, seemingly, at ransom.

To explain further the difference between 'abandonment' *(Tyāga)* and 'renunciation' *(Saṁnyāsa),* the Lord says here that for a man-of-renunciation there is no reaction either to the actions done in the past or to actions undertaken by him in the present. This idea clearly brings out the subtle difference that the *Gītā* makes between *Tyāga* and *Saṁnyāsa.* Earlier we found that *tyāga* capacity in us with which, from moment to moment, we withdraw ourselves from the impulses of our mind; while *Saṁnyāsa* is the total renunciation of the entire "tendencies," both good and bad-from their crystallisation as the "ego."

The *Gītā*-technique for the rehabilitation of man's personality, so beautifully elaborated and exhaustively discussed, when briefly put would be:

(a) the seeker first gets detached from the lower sensuous cravings and passions by identifying himself with the nobler ideals of self-control and moral-perfection;

(b) a mind so conditioned becomes tamer than a mind goaded by sensuality. This purified mind develops in itself the required amount of subtle powers of thinking, of consistent self-application and of steady contemplation;

(c) on realising the Pure 'Be'-ness, all 'becomings' end. To the pure Self there is no becoming; the "tendencies" of the mind *(vāsanā-s)* cannot shackle the Spirit. Its subtle present cannot but be ever Immaculate and Unconditioned.

The 'pleasant," the "unpleasant" and the "mixed" types of reaction *(Karma Phala)* reach only those who have an ego-centric sense of identification with the actions as well as their resultant reactions. Those who abandon *(tyāgī)* both the sense of ego and the anxiety for the action-results are not caught in the clutches of 'reactions-actions'. Memories of the past are the fertile fields where desires are cultivated and it is only in the future that the fruits are borne by the trees of actions. Renouncing our indulgence with the inheritance of the past and leaving all our anxieties for the future, to serve the world as a service to the Lord is abandonment-*tyāga.*

After thus handling the theme of abandonment in general, Kṛṣṇa *now takes up a closer examination of it, dissecting the very component parts that constitute work:*

पञ्चैतानि महाबाहो कारणानि निबोध मे ।
सांख्ये कृतान्ते प्रोक्तानि सिद्धये सर्वकर्मणाम् ।। १३।।

Pañcaitāni mahābāho kāraṇāni nibodha me,
sāṅkhye kṛtānte proktāni siddhaye sarva-karmaṇām.

पञ्च *pañca* = five; एतानि *etāni* = these; महाबाहो *mahābāho* = O mighty-armed; कारणानि *kāraṇāni* = causes; निबोध *nibodha* = learn; मे me = from *me;* सांख्ये *sāṅkhye* = in the *Sāṁkhya;* कृतान्ते *kṛtānte* = which is the end of all actions; प्रोक्तानि *proktāni* = as declared; सिद्धये *siddhaye* = for the accomplishment; सर्व-कर्मणाम् *sarva-karmaṇām* = of all actions.

13. *Learn from Me, O mighty-armed, these five causes for the accomplishment of all actions, as declared in the Sāṅkhya (Upaniṣad) system, which is the end of all actions.*

When *Arjuna* was thus told conclusively that action could be performed without ego-centric desires and clinging attachment to the fruits, as an intelligent enquirer he had every right to ask: "What constitutes an action?" To lay bare the inner essence of action, *Kṛṣṇa* analyses the anatomy of work-the external structure of action, and the physiology of action-the inner inspirations, motives and urges in work.

Addressing *Arjuna* as mighty-armed, *Kṛṣṇa* declares that for the real accomplishment, fulfilment or achievement of an action, five aspects of action are necessarily to be disciplined and marshalled. These five are the "limbs of action" without which no action is ever possible. When these five aspects work in happy co-ordination, the undertaking is assured of the greatest success, be it secular or sacred, material or spiritual. The term "Mighty-armed" is used to invoke the adventurous heroism in *Arjuna,* for, a large share of daring courage, consistency of purpose, faith in oneself and intellectual heroism are necessary, if one is to discipline one's actions and successfully accomplish a thorough cultural development within.

In this stanza, the *Gītācārya* confesses that this enumeration of the aspects that constitute an action is not his own original contribution, but it is exactly what is said in the *Sāṅkhyan* philosophy. The *Sāṅkhyan* philosophy as a separate text no longer exists ... perhaps, here, the word *Sāṅkhyan* indicates only the *Upaniṣad-s.* The existing *Sāṅkhyan* books do not mention these five-fold categories. It is reasonable to suppose that at the time of *Vyāsa* there might have been some books discussing this topic which are now lost to us. However, one thing is clear: that this five-fold division, which the Lord discusses in the following stanzas, faithfully follows the philosophy of the *Gītā* as discussed so far. The *Gītā* has declared that all actions cease when the knowledge of the Self dawns, so that the *Advaita* commentator concludes: " *Vedānta,* which imparts to us knowledge, is the end of actions."

Herein the Lord enumerates ***five factors which are the constituent parts in all actions.***

अधिष्ठानं तथा कर्ता करणं च पृथग्विधम् ।
विविधाश्च पृथक्चेष्टा दैवं चैवात्र पञ्चमम् ।।१४।।

Adhiṣṭhānaṁ tathā kartā karaṇaṁ ca pṛthag-vidhaṁ,
vividhāś-ca pṛthak-ceṣṭā daivaṁ caivātra pañcamaṁ.

अधिष्ठानम् *Adhiṣṭhānam* = the seat or gross body; तथा *tathā* = also; कर्ता *kartā* = the doer (ego): करणम् *karaṇam* = the sense organs of perception; च *ca* = and; पृथग्विधम् *pṛthag-vidham* = various kinds of; विविधा: *vividhāḥ* = various; च *ca* = and; पृथक् *pṛthak* = distinct, different; चेष्टा: *ceṣṭāḥ* = functions (organs of actions, like the senses, the mind etc.); दैवम् *daivam* = the presiding deity; च *ca* = and; एव *eva* = even; अत्र *atra* = here; पञ्चमम् *pañcamam* = the fifth.

14. *The "Seat" (body), the doer (ego), the various kind of organs-of-perception, the different functions of various organs-of-action, and also the presiding deity, the fifth.*

The promise made in the previous stanza is being fulfilled herein and Lord *Kṛṣṇa* enumerates the five component parts that go into the constitution of any "action." We have already discussed that the enumeration as it stands today in this stanza does not correspond to the *Sāṅkhyan* delcaration. Commentators interpret these terms, each slightly differently from the others, and this five-fold division being rather obscure, the various explanations of the commentators are not very helpful to a practical student. However, we can see in these five terms the twenty four-fold division of *Prakṛti,* which the *Sāṅkhyan-s* hold and follow.

Every work is undertaken with the help of the "body" *(Adhiṣṭhānam),* for the body is the gateway for the stimuli to enter as well as for the responses to exist. A body in itself can neither receive the world nor react to it unless there is the "ego" *(Kartā)* functioning in and through it. There must be an intelligent personality, presiding over its own desires, wanting to fulfil them and thus constantly seeking a fulfilment through its body activities. The ego sets the body in continuous activity. When an ego, thus riddled with its own desires, wants to seek its fulfilment in the world of objects outside, it certainly needs "instruments" *(Karaṇam)* of perception. Without these, the inner personality cannot come in contact with the field of enjoyment and find satisfaction in it.

The term "function" *(ceṣṭā)* here has been commented upon by *Śaṅkara* as the physiological activities, known as *Prāṇa, Apāna,* etc. No doubt it is sufficiently explanatory to all students who have a knowledge of the traditions in *Vedāntic* thought. But to a lay student this explanation might be rather confusing. As a result of the physiological activities (*Prāṇa, Apāna,* etc.) the health of the body gets toned up and it must flow out in its own vigour and enthusiasm through the organs-of-action. Thus, for our understanding of these enumerations, we can directly take the term "function" *(Ceṣṭā)* used here as indicating the organs-of-action.

The organs-of-perception are presided over by the five great elements.* These presiding deities are technically called *Deva-s,* and they indicate particular functions and faculties in the sense-organs, such as the "power of vision" of the eye, the "power of audition" in the ears etc. i.e. the sense-organs must have their full vigour and must function properly in order to play their part in any field of work.

Stripping off all these details of explanations, if we re-read the stanza, it merely enumerates the constituent parts of every action. They are:

(1) the body;
(2) the ego;**
(3) the organs-of-perception;
(4) the organs-of-action; and
(5) the five elemental forces.

The stanza is dedicated merely to enumerating these five aspects without which no ego-centric activity is ever possible.

How can these five become the component parts in every human activity?

शरीरवाङ्मनोभिर्यत्कर्म प्रारभते नरः ।
न्याय्यं वा विपरीतं वा पञ्चैते तस्य हेतवः ॥१५॥

Śarīra-vāṅ-manobhir-yat-karma prārabhate naraḥ,
nyāyyaṁ vā viparītaṁ vā pañcaite tasya hetavaḥ.

---

* The eye by Fire, the ears by Space, the tongue by Water, the skin by Air, and the nose by Earth.

** In *Śrī Śaṅkara's* commentary, it is clearly defined as the 'enjoyer,' meaning, the spirit that has identified itself with an intellectual and mental demand for any given gratification.

शरीर-वाङ्-मनोभि: *śarīra-vān-manobhiḥ* = speech and mind; यत् *yat* = whatever; कर्म *karma* = actions; प्रारभते *prārabhate* = performs; नर: *naraḥ* = man; न्याय्यम् *nyāyyam* = right; वा *vā* = or; विपरीतम् *viprītam* = the reverse; वा *vā* = or; पञ्च *pañca* = five; एते *ete* = these; तस्य *tasya* = its; हेतव: *hetavaḥ* = causes.

15. Whatever action a man performs by his body, speech and mind-whether right, or the reverse-these five are its causes.

The items listed above must all come into full play in order to accomplish any work and therefore, these five component parts are called the causes of all actions. To show that there is no exception, the Lord says that whatever action a man might undertake, be it by his body, speech or mind, and that too whether right or wrong, in every expression of action there is the play of all these five essential parts.

These five constitute the equipment of action, and the Spirit, the eternally Actionless, conditioned by the intellectual desires, behaves *as though* it is an ego (Jīva); and this individualised personality, forgetting its own State-of-Perfection demanding satisfaction through sense gratifications, making use of the faculties of sense-enjoyment, strives in the world-of-objects to achieve, to gain, to aggrandise. Here we should not forget, in our haste, to grasp clearly that the five-fold division is the description of "engine under the bonnet" and not of the "petrol"; and yet, "petrol" in itself cannot make the travel pleasant and successful-nor can the "engine" move without the "petrol."

A motor vehicle becomes an automobile only when "petrol" plays through the "engine," and when the driver can, by his faculties, take the vehicle to its destination, which is determined by the demand or the desire of the owner of the vehicle. If this analogy is understood, we can correctly evaluate this portion of *Kṛṣṇa's* enumeration, and can truly appreciate what the Lord means when he says "these five are the causes" of all work.

All these enumerations and explanations of the last two stanzas add up to the conclusion that the 'sense of agency' of the Self is an illusion:

तत्रैवं सति कर्तारमात्मानं केवलं तु यः।
पश्यत्यकृतबुद्धित्वान्न स पश्यति दुर्मतिः ॥१६॥

Tatraivaṁ sati kartāram-ātmānaṁ kevalaṁ tu yaḥ,
paśyaty-akṛta-buddhitvāt-na sa paśyati durmatiḥ.

तत्र-एवम् सति *tatra-evam sati* = this being the case (idiomatic expression); कर्तारम् *kartāram* = as the agent; आत्मानम् *ātmānam* = the Self; केवलम् *Kevalam* = alone; तु *tu* = verily; यः *yaḥ* = who; पश्यति *paśyati* = sees; अकृत बुद्धित्वात् *akṛta-buddhitvāt* = owing to (his) untrained understanding; न *na* = not; सः *saḥ* = he; पश्यति *paśyati* = sees; दुर्मतिः *durmatiḥ* = of perverted intelligence.

16. Now, such being the case, verily he who-owing to his untrained understanding-looks upon his Self, which is "alone" (never conditioned by the "engine"), as the doer, he, of perverted intelligence, sees not.

In the previous stanzas we found that action belongs to the realm-of-*matter,* no doubt *in the presence* of the Spirit. Failing to discriminate thus between the equipments of action and the actionless Spirit, which, in an unhealthy combination between them, comes to manifest as the "actor" (doer), the poor ego-centric personality so born comes to pant and sigh at its own disappointments and failures, or dances and jumps at its own joys and successes. The moment an individual becomes aware of these inner mechanisms and their play, the delusory ego-centric individually ends as it becomes a mere myth of the mind, a delusory phantom of a midsummer, mid-day dream.

'This being the case' (*Tatra evam sati*):–In all such actions, whether good or bad, as undertaken by the body, speech or mind, the essential component parts are the body, ego, organs-of-perception, organs-of-action and the elements; thus all actions belong to matter. But the Spirit, which is the essential nature, in identifying Itself with the matter-vestures, comes to live through the disturbing destinies as the everchanging man. All pangs and joys, all failures and successes, all imperfections and impediments, belong to the ego, which is the Spirit considering Itself as conditioned by these components of action. The Supreme Pure Self (*Kevalam ātmānam*) is misunderstood by the ordinary man to be the actor (*kartāram),* and in the consequent ego-sense, the divinity is forgotten and the individual comes to despair.

The causes of this misunderstanding have been indicated here. Untempered reason *(Akṛta Buddhi)* and perverted mind (Durmati) are the maladjustments in an individual, because of which, right recognition of one's own divinity is not constantly maintained within. The implication of the statement is that, if a seeker can integrate himself-through the process of disciplining his reasoning faculty and guiding his mind away from his intellectual perversities–that individual will come to experience within himself that it is only the five-fold components made up of *matter* that are indulging in the agitations of the outer activity.*

Elucidating the foregoing ideas more vividly, the Lord continues:

यस्य नाहंकृतो भावो बुद्धिर्यस्य न लिप्यते ।
हत्वापि स इमाँल्लोकान्न हन्ति न निबध्यते ।।१७।।

Yasya nāhaṁkṛto bhāvo buddhir-yasya na lipyate,
hatvāpi sa emāṁllokān-na hanti na nibadhyate

यस्य *yasya* = whose; न *na* = not; अहंकृत: *ahaṁkṛtah* = egoistic; भाव: *bhāvaḥ* = the notion; बुद्धि: *buddhiḥ* = intelligence; यस्य *yasya* = of whom; न *na* = not; लिप्यते *lipyate* = is tainted; हत्वा *hatvā* व having slain; अपि *api* = even; स: *saḥ* = he; इमान् imān = these; लोकान् *lokān* = people; न *na* = not; हन्ति = *hanti* = slays; न *na* = not; निबध्यते = nibadhyate = is bound.

17. He who is free from the egoistic notion, whose intelligence is not tainted (by good or evil), though he slays these people, he slays not, nor is he bound (by the action).

---

* Even while they are all dancing round, *Kṛṣṇa,* the spiritual Truth, remains but motionless in the centre of the ring of the dancing crowd, untouched by the *Gopī-s* moving in their esctatic trance. The divinely sweet maidens of *Vraja* dance in thrilled ecstasy because of the maddening music of the Flute-bearer who, by His breath, draws out the 'melody of existence.' To identify ourselves with the Centre is to be the master of the situation; to play among the whirls of dancers is to suffer the fatigue and exhaustion, the thrills and sorrows of the milkmaids of *Vṛndāvana. This is Rāsa-Krīḍā.*

So far we have been told that the realm-of-matter is the field of all activity, and the weeds of sorrows and agitations can grow only therein. The Spirit, the farmer, has an existence independent of this field and yet the farmer, has an existence independent of this field and yet the farmer, in his identification with the self-projections on the field, feels happy or unhappy according to the condition of the field at any given moment.

Similarly, it is our unhealthy contact created by our self-projections on to the matter-envelopments around us that has given rise to the 'ego', which in its turn comes to suffer the buffetings of life. Therefore, *Kṛṣṇa* says that he who is free from the sense of egoism and whose intelligence is not tainted by false values of possession, acquisition, aggrandisement, etc., does no action even though activities take place all around and even through him,"THOUGH HE SLAYS THESE PEOPLE, HE SLAYS NOT."

This does not mean that a man-of-Wisdom, who has withdrawn from his false evaluation of matter, will no longer act in the world. He will not remain like a stone statue. The statement only means, that even while he is acting in the world, to him it is all a self-entertaining game. It is always our ego-centric clinging that leaves impressions *(vāsanā-s)* in our mind and thus actions of the past come to goad us on to more and more activities. A man-of-Perfection who has the necessary discriminative intellect, learns to detach himself and act, and therefore, in him the footprints of the past activities cannot beat out any deepening footpath.

Only when the needle is in contact with the 'record'

can the gramophone thunder forth its tone; only when the ego is in contact with the mind can the individual be propelled forth into the channels of his own *vāsanā-s.* An egoless man of wisdom, when he works in any field, is but expressing the Infinite will and, therefore, in that attitude of total surrender and complete dedication, no action can leave any impression in his mind.

Kṛṣṇa says: "though he kills, he kills not; nor is he bound." Here is the perfect technique of the poet *Vyāsa* who, from the generality of the philosophical statement, suddenly takes the students of the *Gītā* into the immediate problem in hand–the problem of Arjuna in the battlefront, who hesitates to strike, though he is willing to be guided. Arjuna is told that if he can act in the world without identifying himself with the matter-sheaths around him and act continuously in the consciousness of the Divine, even if he kills his kith and kin, teacher and sire, he will not be perpetrating any crime, nor will his actions leave in him murderous *vāsanā-s* distorting his cultural balance and beauty of personality.

If we were to compare the results of the lusty, passionate acts of some self-seeking murderer, with the honourable heroic activities of some devotedly dedicated warrior championing the cause of his country's freedom and independence, we shall easily understand the above assertion of the Lord. The murderer develops *vāsanā-s,* and propelled by his tendencies, he again and again commits heinous crimes and disturbs the society, while the hero on the battle-front, though he too kills many, returns from the battle-front as a more educated, noble, and refined personality. In the former, there is the "ego," and therefore, the foul *vāsanā-s* get registered; while in the latter, the soldier's mind was fixed in his love for the country, and therefore, the murderous activity on the battlefront could not leave in him any ugly mental residue. Once the ego is surrendered in the consciousness of the Divine, no more can the *"bondage of vāsanā-s"* remain in him.*

After thus describing the constituents that make up any action, the Gītācārya *describes the* ***'impulse to karma'*** *and the* ***'basis of karma'.***

ज्ञानं ज्ञेयं परिज्ञाता त्रिविधा कर्मचोदना ।
करणं कर्म कर्तेति त्रिविधः कर्मसंग्रहः ॥१८॥

Jñānaṁ jñeyaṁ parijñātā trividhā karma-codanā,
karaṇam karma karteti trividhaḥ karma-saṁgrahaḥ

ज्ञानम् *Jñānam* = knowledge; ज्ञेयम् *jñeyam* = the knowable (known); परिज्ञाता *parijñātā* = the knower; त्रिविधा *trividhā* = threefold; कर्म-चोदना *karma-codanā* = impulse to action; करणम् *karaṇam* = the organ; कर्म *karma* = the action; कर्ता *kartā* = the agent; इति iti = thus; त्रिविधः *trividhaḥ* = threefold; कर्मसंग्रहः = *karmasaṁgrahaḥ* the basis of action.

18. Knowledge, the known and knower form the threefold "impulse to action"; the organs, the action, the agent, form the three-fold "basis of action."

In the scientific treatment of the subject-matter, Lord *Kṛṣṇa* had already explained the constituent parts that make up an action and also indicated that the entire assemblage is of matter only. Continuing the theme, he is now trying to explain the three-fold impulses that propel

* *Śaṅkara* asks : *'nistraiguṇye pathi, vicaratāṁ ko vidhiḥ ko niṣedhaḥ?'*

activity *(Karma-Codanā)* and also the basis-of-action *(karma-saṁgraha).*

The "impulse to action," according to *Kṛṣṇa* is a threefold arrangement made up of "knowledge *(Jñānam),* the known *(jñeyam)* and the knower (*parijñātā*).: These three are called technically in *Vedānta* as the *'Tripuṭi'.* indicating the 'experiencer,' the 'experienced' and the resultant 'experience'–the 'knower,' the 'known' and the knowledge.' Without these three no knowledge is ever possible, as all "impulses to act" arise out of a play of these three. The *experiencer,* playing in the field of the *experienced,* gains for himself the various *experiences;* and these constitute the secret contents of all actions.*

The "impulse to action" can spring either from the "experiencer," in the form of desire or from the "experienced", in the form of temptation, or from the "experience" in the form of similar memories of some past enjoyments. Beyond these three there is no other "impulse to action" (*Karma-Codanā*).

The "impulse to action," when it has arisen, must also find a field to act in; and the "basis for action" *(Karma-Saṁgraha)* is constituted of the "instruments," the "reaction" and the "agent" (the actor). This "sense of agency" expressed by the ego, can maintain itself only as long as it holds a vivid picture of the "fruits of its action" which it wants to gain. Fruit, meaning the profit or the gain that is intended to be gained by the action, is indicated here by the term 'work' *(Karma).* According to *Śrī Śaṅkarācārya,*

---

* Here we can also use the term *'knowledge'* and say that the *'knower'* playing in a field of the *'known',* gains to himself the various bits of *'Knowledge.'*

'Karma' here means the end.*

When a desirer, the agent, encouraged by this constant attraction towards a satisfying end, want to achieve it, he must necessarily have the instruments-of-action (*Karaṇam*). These instruments include not only the organs-of-perception-and-action, but also the inner equipments of the mind and the intellect. It cannot be very difficult for a student to understand that:

(1) an *agent* having a desire;

(2) maintaining in his mind a clear picture of the *end or* the goal;

(3) with all the necessary instruments to act thereupon, would be the sum total contents of any activity (*Karma-Saṁgraha*).

If any one of the above three items is absent, action cannot take place. These three (*Karaṇam, Kartā* and *Karma*) are together designated as the parts of the "*Karma*-assembly," the "basis of all *Karma-s*"– (*Karma-Saṁgraha*).

Thus having roughly indicated in this stanza the threefold "impulses of action" and the three-fold "basis for action," *Kṛṣṇa* continues to explain in His Song why different people act so differently under different impulses and obey different basis in their actions. He divides each one of them under the three categories of human nature: the 'good' (*Sāttvik*), the 'passionate' (*Rājasik*), and the 'dull' (*Tāmasik*).

The Lord now proceeds to show the threefold distinctions in each one of the above, according to the three predominant–the good, the passionate, and the dull:

---

* That which is sought for, that which is reached through action by the agent.

ज्ञानं कर्म च कर्ता च त्रिधैव गुणभेदतः ।
प्रोच्यते गुणसंख्याने यथावच्छृणु तान्यपि ॥१९॥

Jñānaṁ karma ca kartā ca tridhaiva guṇa-bhedataḥ,
procyate guṇa-saṁkhyāne yathāvat-śṛṇu tānyapi.

ज्ञानम् *Jñānam* = knowledge; कर्म *karma* = action; च *ca* = and; कर्ता *kartā* = actor; च *ca* = and; त्रिधा *tridhā* = three kinds; एव *eva* = only; गुण-भेदतः *guṇa-bhedataḥ* = according to the distinction of temperaments; प्रोच्यते *procyate* = are declared; गुण-संख्याने *guṇa sāṁkhyane* = in the science of temperaments (*guṇa-s*) यथावत् *yathāvat* = duly; शृणु *śṛṇu* = hear; तानि = *tāni* = them; अपि *api* = also.

19. 'Knowledge,' 'action,' and 'actor' are declared in the Science of Temperaments (Guṇa-s) *to be of three kinds only, according to the distinctions of temperaments; hear them also duly.*

As an introduction to what is to follow immediately, here it is said that "knowledge," "action," and the "actor" (agent), all the three, because of the difference of the temperament in the individuals, at the given time of observation, fall under a three-fold division. This classification is being exhaustively explained in the following stanzas.

Guṇa is the preponderance of a given type of temperament in one's inner nature. The human mind and intellect function constantly, but they always come to function under the different "Climatic conditions" within our mind. These varying climates of the mind are called the three *guṇa-s:* the 'good,' the 'passionate' and the 'dull.'

Under each of these temperaments the entire human

personality behaves differently, and, naturally therefore, the permutations and combinations of the varieties make up the infinite types that are available in the world; even within the biography of one and the same personality we find different moods and behaviours at different periods of time, depending entirely upon the occasion, the type of the situtation, the nature of the problem and the kind of challenge the person is called upon to face.

According to the Science of the *guṇa-s,* as enunciated in *Kapila's Sāṁkhya* Yoga, "Knowledge," "Action and "Actor" are each classified under these three categories. They are being enumerated here and *Kṛṣṇa* invites the students of the *Gītā* to listen attentively to them.; It is meaningless, in fact, to ask Arjuna to listen to the discourses, because he was all the time listening to the Lord. The implication must be that the teacher is attracting the special attention of the students because of the importance of the theme.

सर्वभूतेषु येनैकं भावमव्ययमीक्षते ।
अविभक्तं विभक्तेषु तज्ज्ञानं विद्धि सात्त्विकम् ॥२०॥

Sarva-bhūteṣu yenaikam bhāvam-avyaya-mīkṣate,
avibhaktam vibhakteṣu taj-jñānam viddhi sāttvikam

सर्व-भूतेषु *sarva-bhūteṣu* = in all beings; येन *yena* = by which; एकम् *ekam* = one; भावम् *bhāvam* = reality; अव्ययम् *avyayam* = indestructible; ईक्षते *ikṣate* = (one) sees; अविभक्तम् *avibhaktam* = undivided; विभक्तेषु = in the divided; तत् *tat* = that; ज्ञानम् *jñānam* = knowledge; विद्धि *viddhi* = know; सात्त्विकम् *sāttvikam* = *sāttvik* (pure).

20. That by which one sees the one indestructible Reality in all beings, undivided in the divided, know that "knowledge as Sāttvik *(Pure).*

Inasmuch as the constituents of action, namely "knowledge," "work", and the "ego," are under the influences of different moods, each one of them can fall into the three types. We fluctuate among these three *guṇa-s* and the different proportions in which they are mixed in our bosom determine the innumerable types of individuals that we are.

These detailed descriptions of the different types of "knowledge," action and "actor" are given here not for the purpose of judging and classifying others, but for the seeker to *understand himself.* A true student of culture and self-development must try to maintain himself as far as possible, in the *Sāttvik* temperament. By self-analysis, we can diagnose ourselves, and immediately remedy the defects in us.

In this stanza, we have the description of the *Sāttvik* type of "knowledge." The "knowledge" by which the One Imperishable Being is seen in all existence, is *Sāttvik.* Though the forms constituted by the different body-mind-intellect equipments are all different in different living creatures, the *Sāttvik* "knowledge" recognises all of them as the expressions of the One and the same Truth, which is the Essence in all of them.

Just as an electrical engineer recognises the same electricity flowing through all the bulbs, a goldsmith recognises the one metal 'gold in all ornaments, and every one of us is aware of the same cotton in all shirts, so also, the intellect that sees the screen upon which the play of life and the throbs of existence are projected as the Changeless One has the "knowledge" that is *Sāttvik.*

CHART I
THE THRE TYPES OF KNOWLEDGE

THE GOOD *(Sāttvik)*	THE PASSIONATE *(Rājasik)*	THE DULL *(Tāmasik)*
The 'Knowledge,' which can recognise and live constantly the Truth is *sāttvik*. To recognise the flux of things to feel the harmony underlying the unity in diversity of forms and behaviours, to live the awareness of the One Life that pulsates in every bosom, is the genuine achievement of a *sāttvik* intellect.	The 'Knowledge,' which looks upon other living entities as different from one another is passionate: An intellect to which the world is an assortment of various types, behaving under various moods differently, an intellect that recognises the world as made up of an endless incomprehensible plurality, as possessed of 'knowledge' that is *rājasik*.	The 'Knowledge,' which fanatically regards without rhyme or reason, particular path or view the sole end without understanding the path or view correctly and sticks on to it with extreme selfarrogance and egoistic insistence, the 'knowledge' which considers the entire world of things and beings as meant for its owner and his pleasures alone, the 'Knowledge' which fails to recognise anything really existing beyond the little ego, is *tāmasik*.

Undivided in the divided (Avibhaktam Vibhakteṣu): Even if there are a hundred different pots of different shapes and colour, and different sizes, the "space" is the one undivided factor in all these different pots, Bulbs are different but the current that is expressing through them all is the *One* electricity. Waves are different, and yet the same ocean is the reality and the substance in all the waves...Similarly, the *One life* throbs in all, expressing itself differently as Its different manifestations, because of the different constitution in the *matter*-arrangements. The "knowledge" that can recognise the play (*vilāsa*) of this One Principle of Consciousness in and through all the different equipments, is fully *Sāttvik.*

What type of an intellect does the "passionate" possess?

पृथक्त्वेन तु यज्ज्ञानं नानाभावान्पृथग्विधान् ।
वेत्ति सर्वेषु भूतेषु तज्ज्ञानं विद्धि राजसम् ॥२१॥

Pṛthaktvena tu yaj-jñānaṁ nānā-bhāvān-pṛthag-vidhān,
vetti sarveṣu bhūteṣu taj-jñānaṁ viddhi rājasam.

पृथक्त्वेन *pṛthaktvena* = as different from one another; तु *tu* = but; यत् *yat* = which; ज्ञानम् *jñānam* = knowledge; नाना-भावान् *nānā-bhāvān* = various entities; पृथग्विधान् *pṛthag-vidhān* = of distinct kinds; वेत्ति *vetti* = knows; सर्वेषु *sarveṣu* = (in) all; भूतेषु *bhuteṣu* = in beings; तत् *tat* = that; ज्ञानम् *jñānam* = knowledge; विद्धि *viddhi* = know; राजसम् *rājasam.* = *rājasam.* (in terms of passion).

21. *But that "knowledge" which sees in all beings various entities of distinct kinds, (and) as different from one another, know that knowledge as Rājasik (Passionate).*

After having found a description of the 'good,' we have herein an equally complete description of the "knowledge" that is 'passionate' (*Rājasik*).

The "knowledge" that recognises plurality, by reason of separateness, is *Rājasik* in its texture. The "knowledge" of the 'passionate,' ever restless in its energy, considers various entities as different from one another; to the *Rājasik* "knowledge," the world is an assortment of innumerable types of different varieties; the intellect of such a man perceives distinctions among the living creatures, and divides them into different classes-as the animal, the vegetable and the human kingdoms.

The very core of the *Hindu* culture is the recognition of the oneness of the entire living world of creatures. It is the concept of plurality that gives rise to all the passions and desires. And where the plurality is recognised, there the ego has crystallised in the perceiver. Unless the individual stands apart from the world as a separate, distinct entity, he will not be able to recognise a multiple world of separate beings and things.

What then is the nature of "knowledge" of the 'dull'?

यत्तु कृत्स्नवदेकस्मिन्कार्ये सक्तमहैतुकम् ।
अतत्त्वार्थवदल्पं च तत्तामसमुदाहृतम् ।।२२।।

Yat-tu kṛtsnavad-ekasmin-kārye saktama-haitukam,
attattvārthavad-alpaṁ ca tat-tāmasam-udāhṛtam.

यत् *yat* = that which; तु *tu* = but; कृत्स्नवत् *kṛtsnavat* = as if it were the whole; एकस्मिन् *ekasmin* = one single; कार्ये *kārye* = to effect; सक्तम् *saktam* = attached; अहैतुकम्

ahaitukam = without reason अतत्त्व-अर्थवत् *atattva arthavat* = without foundation in Truth; अल्पम् *alpam* = narrow; च *ca* = and; तत् *tat* = that; तामसम् *tāmasam* = *tāmasik* (dark); उदाहृतम् *udāhṛtam.* = is declared.

22. But that "knowledge," which clings to one single effect, as if it were the whole, without reasons, without foundation in truth, and narrow, that is declared to be Tāmasik (dull).

An intellect that has got fumed under the dulling effect of extreme *tamas* clings to one single "effect as though it were the whole, never enquiring into its "cause." The "knowledge" of the dull is painted here as that belonging to the lowest type of spiritual seekers. They are generally fanatic in their faith and in their devotion, in their views and values in life. They never enquire into, and try to discover, the cause of things and happenings; they are unreasonable *(ahaitukam).**

Looking through such a confused intellect loaded with fixed ideas, the dull not only fail to see things as they are, but invaribaly project their own ideas upon the world and judge it all wrongly. In fact, a man of *Tāmasik* intellect views the world as if it is meant for him and his pleasures alone. He totally ignores the Divine Presence, the Infinite Consciousness. The "Knowledge" of the dull is thus circumscribed by its own concept of self-importance, and thus its vision becomes narrow *(alpam)* limited.

To summarise, the "knowledge" of the 'good' (*Sāttvik*) perceives the oneness underlying the Universe; the

---

* *Śaṅkara* comments upon this word and declares it to mean as 'not founded on reason.' The knowledge of the 'dull' recognises only the effects, but ignores the causes.

comprehension of the world; and the understanding of the 'dull' (*Tāmasik*) indicates a highly crystallized, self-centred ego in him, and his view of the world is always perverted and ever false.

In the world outside, we can recognise the sad lot of restlessness and sorrow in those who possess *tāmasik* intellect. The destiny of the *rājasik* type is much better, even though, to the extent it recognises the multiplicity, it has also its own despairs and agitations. But the highest order of intelligence falls under the *sāttvik* type, and the people who possess such intelligence come to live a life of extreme peace and harmony, joy and bliss.

It must again be noted that in this chapter we shall come across similar three-fold divisions in the various aspects of our personal inner life and they are not meant to serve as reckoners to classify *others,* but they are meant to help us to *size ourselves up,* from time to time.

The ***threefold nature of action*** *is now described in the following stanzas:*

नियतं सङ्गरहितमरागद्वेषत: कृतम् ।
अफलप्रेप्सुना कर्म यत्तत्सात्त्विकमुच्यते ।।२३।।

Niyataṁ saṅga-rahitam-arāga-dveṣataḥ kṛtam,
aphala-prepsunā karma yat-tat-sāttvikam-ucyate.

नियतम् *niyatam* = ordained; सङ्ग-रहितम् *saṅga-rahitam* = free from attachment; अराग-द्वेषत: *arāga-dveṣataḥ* = without love or hatred; कृतम् *kṛtam,* = done; अफल-प्रेप्सुना *aphala-prepsunā* = by one not desirous of the fruit; कर्म *karma* = action; यत् yat = which तत् *tat* = that; सात्त्विकम् *sāttvikam* = *sāttvik* (pure); उच्यते *ucyate* = is declared.

23. *An "action" which is ordained, which is free from attachment, which is done without love or hatred, by one who is not desirous of the fruit, that action is declared to be Sāttvik (pure).*

Having so far explained the three types of "knowledge," *Kṛṣṇa* now classifies "actions' *(Karma)* under the same three heads. A *Sāttvik* "action" is the best, productive of peace within and harmony without, in the field of activity, and therefore, it is the purest of the three types of "actions." It is an obligatory action *(Niyatam),* a work that is undertaken for the work's own sake, in an attitude that 'work itself is worship.' Such activities chasten the personality and are ever performed in a spirit of inspiration. Inspired activities naturally surpass the very excellence the actor or the doer is ordinarily capable of. Such an activity is always undertaken without any attachment *(Saṅga-rahitam)* and without any anxiety for gaining any definite end. It is a dedicated activity of love,* and yet, it is not propelled by either love or hatred.

The missionary work undertaken by all prophets and sages are examples in point. We too can recognise the same type of work, which we unconsciously perform on some rare occasions. A typical example that can, at this moment, be remembered is an individual nursing his own wounded limb. As soon as, say, your left toe strikes against some furniture in the house and gets wounded, the entire body bends down to nurse it. Herein, there is neither any special love for the left leg nor any particular extra

---

* An act of love, not merely an act of law; an act of grace, and not a simple act of obligation.

CHART II
THE THREE TYPES OF *'KARMA'* OR WORKS

THE GOOD (*Sāttvik*)	THE PASSIONATE (*Rājasik*)	THE DULL (*Tāmasik*)
Sāttvik actions are those that are one's own obligatory duties towards the society, performed without any clinging attachment to the fruits thereof and that are not motivated by likes and dislikes. He performs these duties just spontancously. He seeks his fulfilment and joy in the very work itself. Such *Sāttvik* actions are undertaken only by men who posses the *Sāttvik* 'Knowledge.'*	*Rājasik* actions are those that are propelled by some desires to be fulfilled, that are performed in a self-centred delusory attitude of *'I-am-the-doer'* vanity, and that are undertaken with great strain and labour on the part of the actor or doer. Such 'actions' are undertaken by the Passionate who possess *rājasik* 'knowledge.'*	*Tāmasik* actions are those that are undertaken without any regard to the consequences thereof, that bring in disaster and sorrow to all around and about the doer, and that sap dry the abilities and vitalities in the doer Himself. Such actions spring from some delusory misconceptions of the goal of life in the individual. Such 'actions' of the dull are generally met with only in persons who possess *tāmasik* 'knowledge.'*

* For an explanation of 'Knowledge,' *Sāttvik, Rājasik* and *Tāmasik* See Chart 1

attachment for it, as compared with other parts of the body. To an individual the whole body is himself, and all parts are equally important; he pervades his whole body.

In the same fashion, an individual with a *Sāttvik* intellect that has recognised the All-pervading One, lives in the Consciousness of the One Reality that permeates the whole Universe, and therefore, to him the leper and the prince, the sick and the healthy, the rich and the poor are so many different parts of his own spiritual personality only. Such an individual serves the world in a sense of self-fulfilment and inspired joy.

Summarising, a *Sāttvik Karma* is a humane action, performed without any attachment, and not motivated either by likes *(Raga)* or dislikes (*Dveṣa*), and undertaken without any desire to enjoy the results thereof. The "action" itself is its fulfilment; a *Sāttvik* man acts, because to remain without doing service is a choking death to him. Such a man of *Sāttvik* "action" alone is a true *brāhmaṇa.*

What is* Rājasik *action ?

यत्तु कामेप्सुना कर्म साहंकारेण वा पुनः।
क्रियते बहुलायासं तद्राजसमुदाहृतम् ।।२४।।

Yattu kāmepsunā karma sāhaṁkāreṇa vā punaḥ,
kriyate bahu-lāyāsaṁ tad-rājasam-udāhṛtam.

यत् *yat* = which; तु *tu* = but; कामेप्सुना *kāmepsunā* = by one longing for desires; कर्म *karma* = action; साहंकारेण *sāhaṁkāreṇa* = with egoism; वा *vā* = or; पुनः *punaḥ* = again; क्रियते *kriyate* = is performed; बहुलायासम् *bahulāyāsam* = with much effort; तत् *tat* = that; राजसम् *rājasam = rājasik (passionate);* उदाहृतम् *udāhṛtam* = is declared.

24. But that "action" which is done by one, longing for desires, or again, done with egoism, or with much effort, is declared to be Rājasik (Passionate).

The "action" of the 'passionate' (*Rājasik*) is that which is undertaken to win one's desires with an extremely insistent "I act" mentality. Always such undertakings are works of heavy toil involving great strain, and all the consequent physical fatigue and mental exhaustion. The individual is impelled to act and struggle by a well-defined and extremely arrogant ego-sense. He works, generally under tension and strain, since he comes to believe that he alone can perform it and nobody else will ever help him. All the time he is exhausted with his own anxieties and fears at the thought whether his goal will ever be achieved, if at all. When an individual works thus with an arrogant ego, and with all its self-centredness, he becomes restless enough to make himself totally exhausted and completely shattered. Such "actions" belong to the category of the passionate (*Rājasik*)

All activities of political leaders, social workers, great industrialists, over-anxious parents, fanatic preachers, proselytising missionaries and blind money-makers, when they are at their best,* are examples of this type.

The characteristic features of actions of the "dull type" (*Tāmasik*) are described hereunder:

अनुबन्धं क्षयं हिंसामनवेक्ष्य च पौरुषम् ।
मोहादारभ्यते कर्म यत्तत्तामसमुच्यते ।।२५।।

---

* For even these can easily fall into the type of the 'dull' (*tāmasik*) which the next stanzas will describe. Here we say, 'when they are at their best.'

Anubandhaṁ kṣayaṁ hiṁsām-anavekṣa ca pauruṣam,
mohād-ārabhyate karma yat-tat-tāmasam-ucyate.

अनुबन्धम् *Anubandham* = consequence; क्षयम् *kṣayam* = loss; हिंसाम् *hiṁsām* = injury; अनवेक्ष्य *anavekṣa** = without regard to; च *ca* = and; पौरुषम् *pauruṣam* = (one's own) ability; मोहात् *mohāt* = from delusion; आरभ्यते *ārabhyate* = is undertaken; कर्म *karma* = action; यत् *yat* = which; तत् *tat* = that; तामसम् *tāmasam = tāmasik (dark);* उच्यते *ucyate* = is declared.

25. That "action" which is undertaken from delusion, without regard for the consequence, loss, injury and ability, is declared to be Tāmasik (dull).

The "actions" *(Karma)* of the 'dull' type (*Tāmasik*) are performed without any consideration for the consequences thereof, without any regard for their loss of power or vitality. Such actors never care for the loss or injury caused to others by their actions, nor do they pay any attention to their own status and ability, when they act. All such careless and irresponsible "actions" (*karma-s*) undertaken merely because of some delusory misconception of the goal, fall under the *Tāmasik* type. Habits of drinking, reckless gambling, corruption, etc., are all examples of the dull (*Tāmasik*) "actions."

Such people have no regard for the consequences of their actions. Ere long, they lose their vitality, and injure all those who are depending upon them. They surrender their dignity and status. their capacities and subtle faculties- all for the sake of their pursuit of a certain delusory goal in life. All they demand is a temporary joy of some sense

* There is another reading अनपेक्ष्य (*Anapekṣya)* in some publications. .. Ed.

gratifications and a tickling satisfaction of some fancy of the hour.

"Action" of this type *(Tāmasik)* immediately provide the performer with a substantial dividend of sorrow. *Rājasik* "action" comparatively takes a longer time to bring its quota of disappointments and sorrows, while *Sāttivk* "action" is always steady and blissful.

*The **three kinds of 'doer' (actors)** are described in the following stanza:*

मुक्तसङ्गोऽनहंवादी धृत्युत्साहसमन्वितः ।
सिद्ध्यसिद्ध्योर्निर्विकारः कर्ता सात्त्विक उच्यते।।२६।।

Mukta-saṅgo-'nahaṁ-vādī dhṛty-utsāha-samanvitaḥ,
siddhya-siddhyor-nirvikāraḥ kartā sāttvika ucyate.

मुक्त-सङ्गः *mukta-saṅgaḥ* = who is free from attachment; अनहंवादी *anaham-vādī* = non-egoistic; धृति-उत्साह-समन्वितः *dhṛti-utsāha samanvitaḥ,* = endowed with firmness and enthusiasm; सिद्धि-असिद्ध्योः = in success or failure; निर्विकारः *nirvikāraḥ* = unaffected; कर्ता *kartā* = an agent; सात्त्विकः *sāttvikaḥ* = *sāttvika* (pure); उच्यते *ucyate* = is declared.

26. *An "agent" who is free from attachment, non-egoistic, endowed with firmness and enthusiasm, and unaffected by success or failure, is called Sāttvik (pure.)*

So far we have a description of the three types of "knowledge" and "Action." The third of the constituents that goes into the make-up of an action is the "Doer," the ego that has the desire to do. Since the three *guṇa-s* come to influence the psychological life and the intellectual perception of all of us, the doer-personality in each one of us must also change its moods and temperaments according to the preponderant *guṇa* that rules the bosom at any given moment of time. Consequently, the "ego" also is classified under three kinds. With this stanza starts the discussion on the three types of "actors" (*kartā*) who act in world outside.

A *Sāttvik* "actor" is the one who is free from attachment to any of his kith and kin (*Mukta-saṅgaḥ*), and non-egoistic (*Anaham-vādin*). He is one who has no clinging attachment to the things and beings around, as he has no such false belief that the world outside will bring to him a desirable fulfilment of his existence. He sincerely feels that he has not done anything spectacular even when he has actually done the greatest good to mankind, because he surrenders his ego-centric individuality to the Lord, through his perfect attunement with the Infinite.

When such an individual-who has destroyed in himself his ego-sense and the consequent sense of attachment-works in the worldly fields of activities, he ever acts with firm resolution (*Dhṛti*), and extreme zeal (*Utsāha*). The term '*Dhṛti*' means "fortitude"-the subtle faculty in man that makes him strive continuously towards a determined goal. When obstacles come his way, it is this faculty of '*Dhṛti*' that discovers for him more and more courage and enthusiasm to face them all, and to continue striving towards the same determined goal. This persevering tendency to push oneself on with the work until one reaches the halls of success, unmindful of the obstacles one might meet with on the path, is called '*Dhṛti*'; and '*Utsāha*' means untiring self-application with dynamic

CHART III
THE THRE TYPES OF DOERS OR ACTORS *(KARTĀ)*

THE GOOD *(Sāttvik)*	THE PASSIONATE *(Rājasik)*	THE DULL *(Tāmasik)*
An actor (does) who has no attachment to the field in which he is acting--who is not egoistic--who is full of fortitude and zeal--who is unmoved by the results of his actions, be they success or failure--such a doer is considered *sāttvik kartā.**	An actor (doer) who is swayed by passions--who ever anxiously ogles at the expected fruit of each action --who is extremely greedy--who acts, bringing often harm to others-- who is impure and sometimes immoral in his means-who is ever buffeted by the joys and sorrows of life--such a doer is considered as a *rājasik kartā.**	An actor (doer) who has no control over his own mental impulses and instincts--who will readily stoop to any vulgarity--who is arrogant and obstinate in his own wrong conclusion--who is deceitful and malicious--who is indolent--who ever lives worried about 'what is to be done' by him--such a 'doer' is considered as a *tāmasik kartā.**

* See Charts I and II for a clearer understanding of threefold classification of 'Knowledge' and 'actor.' Note that the *Sāttvik* 'actor' is propelled by *sāttvik* 'knowledge' and accomplishes 'actions.' So too, the man of passionate nature and the man who falls under the dull category--both of them are propelled by their respective types of 'knowledge' and accomplish the results (actions) thereof,

enthusiasm on the path of achievement, while purusing success.

Lastly, a *Sāttvik* "actor" is one who ever strives unperturbed, both in success and in failure, both in pleasure and in pain. At this moment I can only think of one example of this type of "actor" (*Kārta*): the nurse in the hospital. She has generally no attachment to the patient; she has no ego that she is curing the patient, because she knows that there is the ability of the doctor behind every successful cure. She has fortitude (*Dhṛti*) and enthusiasm (*Utsāha*)-or else she will not be able to continue efficiently in her job. And lastly, she is not concerned with success or failure; she does not rejoice when a patient walks out fully cured, nor does she moan for every patient that dies. She cannot afford such an indulgence. She understands the hospital to be an island of success and failure, of births and deaths, and she is there only to serve.

An "actor" (or agent) of the above type is one who suffers the least dissipation of his energies, and so he successfully manages to bring into the field of his action the mighty total possibilities of a fully unfolded human personality. The *Sāttvik* "agent" strives joyously in *Sāttvik* "actions," guided by his *Sāttvik* "knowledge"; his is the most enduring success, and the world of beings is benefited the most by the inexhaustible rewards of the love-labour of such prophets.

A *Sāttvik* 'actor,' as described above, can be compared with the intelligent attitude, if we may say so, of the domestic broom-stick. No doubt, it is the broom that cleans the house and keeps it spick and span; but by itself it is helpless, and can only lie reclined, neglected and inert in its own corner. But while it is serving to clean the house, in its right understanding, it must realise that if its softer end is efficiently serving to clean the field, it is because its stouter end is in the delicate hands of the mother of the house.

A *Sāttvik Kartā* realises that in all his actions, his body, mind and intellect come into play and serve the world only because the Spirit, the Infinite, is in contact with them. The equipments of matter are as helpless as a broomstick left in a corner. Whenever the body functions, the mind-intellect-equipment throbs and heaves in its pursuit of the new ideals and achievements. And this is because of the Life which thrills them into their respective expressions.

If the broomstick, in its foolishness, forgets the 'will of the mother' and does not totally surrender into her hands to become a vehicle for her will to play through, it is harmful to the broomstick. Generally, we find that whenever a broom misbehaves in the hands of the 'mother', she invariably upturns the broomstick and bangs its head against the floor (to make the chords around it more tight.) The facilties of the intellect, the beauties of the heart, the vitality of the body, are all vehicles for the Sacred Will of the Spirit to sing through. If the vehicles are not properly disciplined, and if they do not come to surrender totally to the Infinite, the Lord, they get broken and shattered.

A *Sāttvik* "doer" is the one who is ever conscious of the touch of the Infinite Light in all his activities.

Who is the Rājasik 'doer'?

रागी कर्मफलप्रेप्सुर्लुब्धो हिंसात्मकोऽशुचिः।
हर्षशोकान्वितः कर्ता राजसः परिकीर्तितः ।।२७।।

Rāgī karmaphala-prepsur-lubdho hiṁsātmako' śuciḥ
harṣa-śokānvitaḥ kartā rājasaḥ parikīrtitaḥ

रागी *rāgī* = passionate; कर्म-फलप्रेप्सुः *karma-phala-prepsuḥ* = desirous of fruits of actions; लुब्धः *lubdhaḥ* = greedy; हिंसात्मकः *himsātmakaḥ* = cruel; अशुचिः *aśuciḥ* = impure; हर्ष-शोकान्वितः *harṣa-sokānvitaḥ* = full of delight and grief; कर्ता *kartā* = agent; राजसः *rājasaḥ* = *rājasik* (passionate); परिकीर्तितः *parikīrtitaḥ* = is called.

27. Passionate, desiring to gain the fruits-of-actions greedy, harmful, impure, full of delight and grief, such an "agent" is said to be Rājasik (passionate).

A "doer" belonging to the passionate type is being exhaustively painted here. He is full of desires, passions and attachments, and he tenaciously clings on to some wished-for gain or goal. He is swayed by passion *(rāgī)* and eagerly seeks the fruit of his work. He is ever greedy *(Lubdhaḥ)* in the sense that such a *Rājasik* "doer" is never satisfied with what he gains and greedily thirsts for more. His thirst is insatiable because his desires multiply from moment to moment.

When a man, full of desires and passions, works with mounting greed, he naturally becomes very malignant (*Hiṁsātmakaḥ*) in his programmes of purusuit. He never hesitates even to injure another, if such injury were to win his end. He is blind to the amount of sorrow he might bring to others; he is concerned only with the realisation of his ulterior motives. When a man of this type (with the above qualities) becomes maliciously resolved to gain his own ends, it is but natural that he becomes impure (*Aśuciḥ*), meaning "immoral."

Even unrighteous methods and vulgar immoralities are no ban to such a "doer" and he will pursue them, if his particular desire can be fulfilled thereby. He may ordinarily be quite a moral and righteous man, but the beauty of his composure and the steadiness of his morality, expressed during his quieter moments, all fly away as brilliant splinters when the sledge hammer of his greed and passion, vengeful plans and malignant schemes, thuds upon his heart.

It is but natural that such a passionate "doer," when he acts in his blinding desires, comes to live, all through his embodied existence, a sad life of agitations, moved by joys and sorrows, "full of delight and grief." (*Harṣa-śoka-anvitaḥ*). This completes the picture of a man who is a 'passionate' (*Rājasik*) "doer."

And **how does a *Tāmasik* 'doer' function** in the field of activity ?

अयुक्तः प्राकृतः स्तब्धः शठो नैष्कृतिकोऽलसः।
विषादी दीर्घसूत्री च कर्ता तामस उच्यते ॥२८॥

Ayuktaḥ prākṛtaḥ stabdhaḥ śaṭho naiṣkṛtiko-'lasaḥ,
viṣādī dīrgha-sūtrī ca kartā tāmasa ucyate.

अयुक्तः *ayuktaḥ* = unsteady; प्राकृतः *prākṛtaḥ* = vulgar; स्तब्धः *stabdhaḥ* = unbending; शठः *śaṭhaḥ* = cheating; नैष्कृतिकः *naiṣkṛtikah* = malicious; अलसः *alasaḥ* = lazy; विषादी *viṣādī* = despondent; दीर्घसूत्री *dīrgha-sūtrī* = procrastinating (one who defers action); च *ca* = and; कर्ता *kartā* = agent; तामसः *tāmasaḥ* = *tāmasik* उच्यते (dull): ucyate = is said

28. Unsteady, vulgar, unbending, cheating, malicious, lazy, despondent, and procrastinating, such an "agent is said to be *Tāmasik (dull).*

Here we have a description of a *Tāmasik* "doer" pursuing his work motivated by his *Tāmasik* "knowledge" and expressing himself through his *Tāmasik* "actions."

Uncontrolled (*Ayuktaḥ*):- A "doer" who has no control over himself, and therefore, is ever unsteady in his application, is of the *Tāmasik* type. He becomes unbalanced in his activities, becuase his mind does not obey the warnings of his intellect. A yukta-mind is one which is obedient to and perfectly under the control of the intellect. A *tāmasik* man is uncultured inasmuch as he acts in the world, spurred by the impulses and instincts of his own mind. The glory of a cultured man comes out only when he brings the impulsive storms of his mind under the chastening control and intelligent guidance of his intellect. He is *Ayuktaḥ,* who behaves with no control over his own animal impulses and low instincts. When such an individual acts in the world, he cannot but behave as a vulgar man (*Prākṛtaḥ*).

When an individual thus acts, if anyone around him were to show an intellectual mirror, he will never admit the reflected vulgarities as his own, nor will he acknowledge his way of living as base and licentious. He is arrogant and obstinate (*Stabdhaḥ*) and in his stubborn nature he will not lend himslef to be persuaded to act more honourably.*

Dishonest (*Śaṭhaḥ*):- He becomes dishonest. He

* *Para-vṛtti-chedanaparaḥ*-He maintain a malicious attitude towards anybody who tries to come and interefere in the way of his desire-gratifications.

becomes extremely deceitful. Herein the dishonesty, or deceitfulness, arises out of his incapacity to see any point-of-view other than the false conclusions he has arrived at. Such an individual is not a dependable character, for he conceals his real motives and purpose and secretly works out his programmes which generally bring about a lot of sorrow to all around him.

Malicious (*Naiṣkṛtikaḥ*) :- The term describes, according to *Śaṅkara,* one who is bent upon creating quarrels and disputes among people. With a vengefulness, such a person pursues his adversary to destory him. Family fueds etc., are typical examples.

***Indolent* (*Alasaḥ*) :-** The "dull doer" is a very indolent man spending his time in over-indulgence. He is an idler, for he avoids all creative endeavours and productive efforts, if by deceit or cunning, he can easily and readily procure enjoyable chances and pleasure-goods. He pursues such a path, however immoral it may be. He is a social parasite; he enjoys and consumes without striving and producing. He puts forth no effort; drowsiness of intellect that renders him incapable of correct thinking is a typical feature. The three brothers, from *Laṅkā,* in fact, represent these three types of "doers." Of them, Kumbhakarṇa, who sleeps six months and wakes up only to spend the rest of the six months in eating, is symbolic of a *Tāmasik* "doer."*

***Despodent* (*Viṣādī*) :-** He is one who will not meet the challenge of life squarely. He has neither the vitality nor the stamina to stand up against the challenges of life.

* *Rāvaṇa,* the mighty, represents the *rājasik kartā,* and *Vibhiśana,* the devout, is an example of *Sāttvik kartā.*

This is because his over-indulgent nature has sapped up all his vitality and courage to meet life. Invariably, he spends his time complaining of men and things around him and wishes for a secure spot in the world? where he can be away from all obstacles so that he may peacefully continue satisfying his endless thirst for sensuous enjoyments.

***Procrastinater* (*Dīrgha-sūtrī*) :-** An individual so benumbed in his inner nature, slowly gathers within himself an incapacity to arrive at any firm judgement. Even if he comes to any vague decision, he has not the will to continue the consistent pursuit of his judgement. Indolent as he is by nature, more often than not, he postpones the right activity until it is too late. This procrastinating tendency is natural to a *Tāmasik* "actor." The term *dīrgha-sūtrī* has been interpreted by some commentators as "harbouring deep and long (*dīrgha*) vengeance against others (*sūtra*)," which is also not inappropriate in the context of the thought development in this stanza.

Thus one who is unsteady, vulgar, arrogant, deceitful, malicious, indolent, despondent and procrastinating, belongs to the 'dullest' type of "agents" available in the fields of human endeavour. This and the two preceding stanzas provide us with three beautifully framed mental pictures, bringing out in all details the *Sāttvik*, the *Rājasik* and *Tāmasik* type of "doers" available in the world. As we have already emphasised, these pictures are not yardsticks to classify others, but are meant for the seekers to observe themselves. Whenever a true seeker discovers symptoms of *Tamas* and *Rajas* growing in him he should take notice of them at once and consciously strive to regain his *Sāttvik* beauty.

According to the predominating guna, "understading" and "fortitude" also can fall under a three-fold classification- says Kṛṣṇa:

बुध्देर्भेदं धृतेश्चैव गुणतस्त्रिविधं श्रृणु ।
प्रोच्यमानमशेषेण पृथक्त्वेन धनंजय ॥२९॥

Buddher-bhedaṁ dhṛteś-caiva guṇatas-trividhaṁ śṛṇu,
procya-mānam-aśeṣeṇa pṛthak-tvena dhanañjaya.

बुध्देः *buddheḥ* = of understanding; भेदम् *bhedam* = division; धृतेः *dhṛteḥ* = of fortitude; च *ca* = and; एव *eva* = even; गुणतः *guṇataḥ* = according to qualities (modes or moods); त्रिविधम् *trividham* = threefold; श्रृणु *śṛṇu* = hear; प्रोच्यमानम् *procya-mānam* = as declare; अशेषेण *aśeṣeṇa* = fully; पृथक्त्वेन *pṛthak-tvena* = severally; धनंजय *dhanañjaya* = O *dhanañjaya.*

29. *Hear (you) the three-fold division of "understanding" and "fortitude" (made) to the qualities, as I declare them fully and severally,* O Dhanañjaya

'Work,' no doubt, is constituted of the three factors; the "knowledge," the "action" and the "actor." Each of these three factors was shown to fall under a three-fold classification and all these classifications were described in the foregoing nine stanzas.* When an actor, guided by his knowledge, acts in the world, no doubt, manifestation of work takes place. But underlying these three, are two factors which supply the fuel and the motive force in all sustained endeavours. They are "understanding" (*Buddhi*) and "fortitude" (*Dhṛti*)

* As ready help for your memory, see previous charts.

The former, *buddhi,* or "understanding," means "the intellectual capacity in the individual to grasp what is happening around him." "Fortitude" *(Dhṛti)* is "the faculty of constantly keeping one idea in the mind and consistently working it out to its logical end"; consistency of purpose and self-application, without allowing oneself to be tossed about hither and thither like a dry leaf at the mercy of a fickle breeze, is called "fortitude."

The operative part in every field of activity is controlled and guided by our intellectual capacity of "understanding," and faithful consistency of purpose, "fortitude." This stanza is an introduction to a scientific discussion of these two faculties (*Buddhi* and *Dhṛti*) and their three-fold classification.

Kṛṣṇa invites again the special attendion of Arjuna to these classifications, which he is going to discuss severally.

What is *Sāttvik* understanding?

प्रवृत्तिं च निवृत्तिं च कार्याकार्ये भयाभये ।
बन्धं मोक्षं च या वेत्ति बुद्धिः सा पार्थ सात्त्विकी ॥३०॥

Pravṛttiṁ ca nivṛttiṁ ca
kāryā-kārye bhayā-bhaye,
bandhaṁ mokṣaṁ ca yā vetti
buddhiḥ sā pārtha sāttvikī.

प्रवृत्तिम् *pravṛttim* = action, the path of work; च *ca* = and; निवृत्तिम् *nivṛttim* = the path of renunciation; च *ca* = and; कार्य-अकार्ये *kārya-akārye* = what ought to be done and what ought not to be done; भय-अभये *bhaya-abhaye* = fear and fearlessness; बन्धम् *bandham* = bondage; मोक्षम् *mokṣam* = liberation; च *ca* = and; या *yā* = that; वेत्ति *vetti* = knows

CHART IV
THE THRE TYPES OF UNDERSTANDING *(BUDDHI)**

THE GOOD *(Sāttvik)*	THE PASSIONATE *(Rājasik)*	THE DULL *(Tāmasik)*
The 'understanding' that can readily judge things that are to be done *(pravṛtti)* and things that are to be renounced or avoided *(nivṛtti)*-- that correctly discerns what ought to be done *(kāryam)* and what ought not to be done *(a-kāryam)*--that can undertand fear and fearlessness--is considered as the *sāttvik buddhi* an 'understanding' of Purity.	The 'understanding' that erroneously conceives both the right and the wrong, that falsely judges what should be done and what should not be done (due to its false egoistic preconception)--is considered as the *rājasik buddhi:* an 'understanding' of Energy.	The 'understanding' that deems the wrong as the right, reversing every value-involved in darkness (ignorance) and, therefore, sees all things in a perverted way, ever contrary to the truth--is considered as the *tāmasik buddhi:* an 'understanding' of Darkness.

* 'Understanding' is intellectual ability with which one can neadily judge rightly the rising situation and the received stimuli. Without this correct judgement, one's responses cannot be appropriate. Sorrows of life, failures in our activities, are all due to the absence of the right and efficient type of 'understanding' in us. *Sāttvik: buddhi* never fails. *Rājasik buddhi:* can fail. But the *tāmasik buddhi:* often fails--and rarely succeeds.

बुद्धिः *buddhiḥ* = understanding; सा *sā* = that; पार्थ *pārtha* = O *pārtha;* सात्त्विकी *sāttvikī* = (of) *sāttvik* (nature)

30. That which knows the paths of work and renunciation, what ought to be done and what ought not to be done, fear and fearlessness, bondage and liberation, that "understanding" is *Sāttvik* (*pure*), O Pārtha.

The intellect may be considered as having the best type of "understanding" if it can readily discriminate among beings and situations in its field of activity. The intellect has various functions-observing, analysing, classifying, willing, wishing, remembering and host of others-and yet, we find that the one faculty essential in all of them is the "power of discrimination." Without 'discrimination,' neither observation nor classification, neither understanding nor judgement, is ever possible. Essentially, therefore, the function of the intellect is "discrimination," which is otherwise called the faculty of "right understanding."

An "understanding" (*Buddhi*) which is capable of clearly discriminating between the *right* field of pursuit and the *wrong* field of false proposition, is the highest type of "understanding." The individual must have the nerve to pursue the *right* path, and also the heroism to defect from all *wrong* fields of futile endeavour. In short, true "understanding" has a ready ability to discriminate between actions that are to be pursued (*Pravṛtti*) and actions that are to be shunned (*Nivṛtti*).

An intellect that can discriminate between the true and the false types of work must also be able to function in judging correctly *"what is right and what is wrong."* Every moment, we are called upon to decide what responses should be made to the flux of happenings and challenges that continuously take place around us. A *Sāttvik Buddhi* always helps us to arrive at the correct judgement. A person in a mood of anger or with a wounded vanity, suddenly resigns his job only to regret thereafter, the folly of his action. His capacity to judge rightly was mutilated by his bad temper of the moment, or by his exaggerated vanity, and so he comes to regret. *Arjuna* himself had come to a state of mental hysteria when he complained that his power of judgement had been lost, mainly because of his inordinate attachment to his kith and kin.

What is to be feared and what is not be feared (*bhaya-abhaya*)-"Fools rush in where angels fear to tread." Men of indiscrimination, in their false evaluation of the sense-world, hug on to delusory objects and things, fearing nothing from them, and yet, they fear to read and understand philosophy, to strive and to experience the Infinite. A true intellect must have the right "understanding" to discriminate between what is to be feared and what is not to be feared. The typical example to illustrate this is strikingly brought out in the *Rāmāyaṇa* where we find that the invincible hero, *Śrī Rāmacandra.* with superhuman courage, faces almost alone the mighty tyrant of *Laṅka* to win *Sītā* back, while the very same warrior *Śrī Rāma* readily meets with the demand of an ordinary *dhobi* (washer-man) who accuses the same *Sītā.* This is an example of the best type of 'understanding which knows when to be fearless and when to be fearful.

***Bondage and Liberation* (*Bandham Mokṣam ca*):-** If the "understanding" is clear, we can easily recognise the tendencies in our make-up that entangle the Higher in us, and curtail its fuller play. To observe and analyse ourselves with the required detachment, and to evaluate critically our psychological behaviours and intellectual attitudes in life, is not easy; it is possible only for those who are endowed with a well-cultivated *Sāttvik* "understanding." If we cultivate *Sāttvik* "understanding," it can not only diagnose for us the false values and wrong emotions that work in us, but also intuitively discover the processes of unwinding ourselves from these cruel *vāsanā-s*, and help us to regain our personality-freedom from these subjective entanglements.

To summarise: the *Sāttvik Buddhi* is defined as one which makes known to us what type of work is to be done and what type of work is to be renounced, which distinguishes the right from the wrong, which knows what is to be feared and what is to be faced fearlessly, which shows us the causes of our own present ugliness in life and explains to us the remedies for the same.

Proper "understanding" can make a garden in a desert, can churn out pure success from every threat of failure. Without "understanding" and "fortitude," even the best of chances will become utter disaster. Right "understanding" can convert the greatest of tragedies into chances for ushering in a propserous destiny. To elucidate this idea, elderly *Mahātmā-s* generally tell us a story.

Once upon a time there was a kingdom on a river bank, and on the opposite bank was a range of hills with thick forest infested with wild man eaters. In this kindgom, the ruling prince was always elected, and each one reigned the country for five years. At the end of every fifth year, on an auspicious hour, the then *Rājā* was ceremoniously conducted to the banks of the river taken across the river in a royal boat, and left in the jungle to be mauled and killed by the man-eaters.

Indiscriminate and foolish ones, elected by the public, joyously came to the throne and forgetful to their appointment with death on the opposite bank, indulged in sensuality and lived on. And all of them met with the inevitable end in time, in their licentiousness.

Then came *Śrī Buddhimān*, who was elected to the throne. As usual, the representative and noblemen among the subject announced after the election that he was the *Rājā* and for the next five years he would be implicitly obeyed by all the subject. *Śrī Buddhimān,* as soon as he ascended the throne, first of all ordered his entire army to move on to the other bank and to clear the whole jungle. The treasury reserves were emptied in constructing a new city across the river, on the other shore. He ordered all the great industrialists and businessmen to occupy the new capital, and at the end of the fifth year, according to the tradition of the kindgom, when he was ordered to retire to the other bank, he in regal splendour and glory, reached his new kingdom, all ready by right 'understanding.'

An intellect that can thus discriminate properly, plan intelligenly, execute diligently can also prepare a vast kingdom for the hereafter-a kingdom of joy, success and prosperity. Such an 'understanding' is considered by *Kṛṣṇa* as *Sāttvik* 'understanding.

What is Rājasik understanding?

यया धर्ममधर्मं च कार्यं चाकार्यमेव च ।
अयथावत्प्रजानाति बुद्धिः सा पार्थ राजसी ।।३१।।

Yayā dharmam-adharmaṁ ca kāryaṁ cākāryam-eva ca.
ayathāvat-prajānāti buddhiḥ sā pārtha rājasī

यया *yayā* = which; धर्मम् *dharmam* = dharma; अधर्मम् *adharmam* = *adharma;* च *ca* = and; कार्यम् *kāryam* = what ought to be done: च *ca* = and; अकार्यम् *akāryam* = what ought not to be done; एव *eva* = even; च *ca* = and; अयथावत् *ayathāvat* = wrongly; प्रजानाति *prajānāti* = understands; बुद्धि: *buddhiḥ* = intellect; सा *sā* = that; पार्थ = *O pārtha;* राजसी *rājasī* = *rājasīk* (passionate).

31. That by which one wrongly understands *Dharma* and *Adharma* and also what ought to be done and what ought not to be done, that intellect (understanding), O pārtha, is *Rājasīk (passionate).*

The "understanding" of the passionate (*Rājasīk*) comes to judge the righteous (*Dharma*) and the unrighteous (*Adharma*), what is to be done and what is not to be done in a slightly perverted manner *(Ayathāvat).* Such *Rājasīk* "understading" cannot reach right judgements, because it is invariably coloured by its own pre-conceived notions and powerful likes and dislikes.

Śrī Ānandagiri, in his notes on Śāṅkara's commentary brings out a subtle difference between the two pairs of phrases used in the stanza, righteous and the unrighteous (*dharma and adharma*), and what ought to be done and what ought not to be done (*kārya and akārya*). He says: *Dharma* and *adharma* here spoken of refer to "*apūrva*," that is, the forms which actions assume after their performance till their effects become perceptible; whereas *kārya* and *akārya* refer to performance or non-performance of the acts. Hence, the tautology.'

What is *Tāmasik* understanding?

अधर्मं धर्ममिति या मन्यते तमसावृता ।
सर्वार्थान्विपरीतांश्च बुद्धिः सा पार्थ तामसी ।।३२।।

Adharmaṁ dharmam-iti yā manyate tamasā-vṛtā,
sarvārthān-viparītāṁś-ca buddhiḥ sā pārtha tāmasī.

अधर्मम् *adharmam* = *adharma*; धर्मम् *dharmam* = dharma; इति *iti* = *that;* या *yā* = which; मन्यते *manyate* = thinks; तमसा *tamasā* = in darkness; आवृता *āvṛtā* = enveloped; सर्वार्थान् *sarvārthān* = all things; विपरीतान् *viparītān* = perverted; च *ca* = and; बुद्धिः *buddhiḥ* = intellect; सा *sā* = that; पार्थ = *O pārtha;* तामसी *tāmasī* = *tāmasik* (dull).

32. That which, enveloped in darkness, sees Adharma as Dharma, and all things perverted, that intellect (understanding), O Pārtha, *is Tāmasik (dull).*

The type of "understanding" which brings sorrow to everyone including the individual himself, is the "understanding" of the 'dull' (*Tāmasik).* Actually it is no "understanding" at all; it can, at best, be called only a chronic bundle of misunderstandings. Such an intellect runs into its own conclusions; but unfortunately, it always lands up with wrong conclusions only. It has such a totally perverted "understanding" that it recognises "*A-dharma*" as "*Dharma,*" the 'right' as 'wrong.' This faculty of coming to wrong judgements is amply seen in the dull, because their entire reasoning capacity is enveloped by complete darkness and egoistic drunkenness.

Discussing the three types of "fortitude," Lord Kṛṣṇa *continues:*

धृत्या यया धारयते मनःप्राणेन्द्रियक्रियाः ।
योगेनाव्यभिचारिण्या धृतिः सा पार्थ सात्त्विकी ॥३३॥

Dhṛtyā *yayā dhārayate manaḥ-prāṇendriya-kriyāḥ,*
yogenā-vyabhi-cāriṇyā dhṛtiḥ sā pārtha sāttvikī.

धृत्या *Dhṛtyā* = by firmness: यया *yayā* = (by) which; धारयते *dharayate* = holds; मनः प्राण इन्द्रिय क्रियाः *manaḥ prāṇa indriya kriyāḥ*= the functions of the mind, the *prāṇa* and the senses: योगेन *yogena* = by *yoga*; अव्यभिचारिण्या *avyabhicāriṇyā* = unswerving; धृतिः *dhṛtiḥ* = fortitude; सा *sā* = that; पार्थ *pārtha* = *O pārtha;* सात्त्विकी *sāttvikī* = *sāttvik.*

33. The unwavering "fortitude" by which through Yoga, the functions of the mind, the Prāṇa and the senses are restrained, that "fortitude," O Pārtha, *is Sāttvik (pure).*

In this section of three stanzas, we get a description of the three types of "fortitude" (*Dhṛti*). There is no correct English equivalent for this word *dhṛti* even though steadiness. consistency, fortitude, are some of the terms used by the great translators. Each one of them is incomplete without the others and one should admit that even all of them put together are but a shade less than the suggestions of the original *dhṛti* in *Samskṛta.*

Dhṛti is that power within ourselves by which we constantly see the goal we want to achieve, and while striving towards it, *Dhṛti* discovers for us the necessary constancy of purpose to pursue the path, in spite of all the mounting obstacles that arise on the way. *Dhṛti* paints the idea, maintains it constantly in our vision, makes us steadily strive towards it, and when obstacles come, *Dhṛti* *mobilises* secret powers within us to face them all

CHART V
THE THRE KINDS OF 'FORTITUDE' *(DHṚTI)**

THE GOOD *(Sāttvik)*	THE PASSIONATE *(Rājasik)*	THE DULL *(Tāmasik)*
The 'fortitude' by which one, through (concentration), *Yoga* controls steadily the ativities of the mind, sense-organs of action *(prāṇendriyas)* and the organs of perception *(indriya-s)* is the 'pure' type of 'fortitude.'	The 'fortitude' by which one holds on firmly with attachment to duty *(dharma),* pleasure *(karma),* and wealth *(artha)*-- ever desirous of coming to enjoy the future rewards of joy promised by them (fruits of action)--is of the 'passionate' type of 'fortitude.'	The 'fortitude' by which a foolish man does not abandon sleep (non-apprehension of reality), fear (fancied fear of something to happen), grief (for something already happened), depression and arrogance while living the present--is the 'dull' type of 'fortitude.'

* See the previous four charts. If read together, the charts should give a clear picture of the uniqueness of the three personalities namely, *sattva, rajas,* and *tamas.*

courageously, heroically, and steadily. We shall use the term "fortitude" to indicate all the abovementioned suggestions implied in the term *Dhṛti.*

This secret fire in man that makes him glow in life and rockets him to spectacular achievements is not generally found in those who have no control over themselves and are voluptuously indulging in sensuous fields. A dissipated individual who has drained off his energy through wrong-thinking and false-living, shall discover no *Dhṛti* in himself. The subtle faculty of "fortitude" is being analysed and classified here, under the three main heads; the 'good' *(Sāttvik),* the 'passionate' (*Rājasik*) and the 'dull' (*Tāmasik*). But in all of them, it is interesting to note, *Dhṛti* stands for "the constancy of purpose" with which every individual pursues his field of endeavour chosen for him, with his own "understanding" (Buddhi). The constancy with which one steadily controls one's mind and sense-organs and their activities, through single-pointed attention and faithful concentration upon a given point-of-contemplation, is the *Dhṛti* of the *Sāttvik* type.

Mind alone can control the organs-of-action *(Karma-indriya-s)* and the organs-of- perception (*Jñāna-indriya-s*). To dissuade the organs-of-action and perception from their false pursuits of the ephemeral joys and the consequent dissipations, the mind must have some fixed source to draw its energies and satisfactions from. Without fixing the mind upon something nobler and higher, we cannot detach it from its present pursuits. Therefore, *Kṛṣṇa* insists that *Yoga* is unavoidable.

With faithful contemplation upon the Self, the mind

gains in steadiness and equipoise, peace and satisfaction, and therefore, it develops a capacity to rule over the sense-organs. But all these achievements are possible only when the inward personality can constantly supply a steady stream of *Dhṛti.* Constancy in endeavour and consistency of purpose or "fortitude" that is expressed in any field of activity, becomes *Sāttvik Dhṛti* when constituted as described above.

What is Rājasīk dhṛti?

यया तु धर्मकामार्थान्धृत्या धारयतेऽर्जुन ।
प्रसङ्गेन फलाकाङ्क्षी धृतिः सा पार्थ राजसी ।।३४।।

Yayā tu dharma-kāmārthān-dhṛtyā dhārayate-'rjuna.
prasaṅgena phalā-kāṅkṣī dhṛtiḥ sā pārtha rājasī.

यया *yayā* = (by) which: तु *tu* = but; धर्म-काम-अर्थान् = duty, pleasure, and wealth; धृत्या *dhṛtyā* = by fortitude; धारयते *dhārayate* = holds; अर्जुन *Arjuna* = *O Arjuna;* प्रसङ्गेन *prasaṅgena* = from attachment; फल आकाङ्क्षी *phala-ākāṅkṣī* = desirous of the fruits of actions; धृतिः *dhṛtiḥ* = fortitude; सा *sā* = that; पार्थ *pārtha* = *O pārtha;* राजसी *rājasī.* = *rājasī* (passionate).

34. But the fortitude, O Arjuna, by which one holds fast to duty, pleasure and wealth, from attachment and craving for the fruits-of-actions, O Pārtha, is Rājasik. (Passionate).

The constancy with which a person holds fast to duty (*Dharma*), wealth (*Artha*) and pleasure (*Kāma*), encouraged by his growing desire to enjoy the fruit of each of them, is the steadiness or "fortitude" of the *Rājasik* type. It is interesting to note that in the enumeration *Kṛṣṇa* avoids

Mokṣa and only takes the first three of the "four ends of man" (*Puruṣārtha*), for, a *Rājasik* man is satisfied with the other fields of self-effort and has no demand for spiritual liberation. The constancy of pursuit of such an individual will be in these three fields of duty, wealth and pleasure, and he will be pursuing one or the other of them with an extreme desire to enjoy the resultant satisfactions. He follows *Dharma* only to gain the heavens; he pursues Artha so that he may have power in this life; and he pursues *Kāma* with a firm belief and faith that sensuous objects can give him all satisfactions in life. The steadiness with which one with such an "understanding" would strive and work in these fields is classified as *Rājasik* Dhṛti.

What is *Tāmasik dhṛti?*

यया स्वप्नं भयं शोकं विषादं मदमेव च ।
न विमुञ्चति दुर्मेधा धृतिः सा पार्थ तामसी ।।३५।।

Yayā svapnaṁ bhayaṁ śokaṁ viṣādaṁ madam-eva ca,
na vimuñcati durmedhā dhṛtiḥ sā pārtha tāmasī.

यया *yayā* = (consistency) by which: स्वप्नम् *svapnam* = sleep; भयम् bhayam = fear; शोकम् *śokam* = विषादम् *viṣādam* = depression; मदम् *madam* = conceit or arrogance; एव *eva* = indeed; च *ca* = and; न *na* = not; विमुञ्चति *vimuñcati* = abandons; दुर्मेधाः *durmedhāḥ* = a stupid man; धृतिः *dhṛtiḥ* = fortitude; सा *sā* = that; पार्थ *pārtha = O pārtha;* तामसी *tāmasī.* = *tāmasīk* (dull).

35. *The 'constancy' because of which a stupid man does not abandon sleep, fear, grief, depression, and also arrogance(conceit),* O Pārtha, is *Tāmasik (dull) "fortitude,".*

CHART VI
THE THRE KINDS OF 'HAPPINESS'

THE GOOD (*Sāttvik*)	THE PASSIONATE (*Rājasik*)	THE DULL (*Tāmasik*)
The *Sāttvik* happiness' is the arising out of the inner self-control and consequent self-perfection which, though it looks painful and arduous in the beginning, is enduring in the long run, in contrast with the fleeting joys provided by sense-ticklings. The result of inner discipline and contemplation brings about tranquillity *(prasād)* in the intellect, and from this tranquillity of the intellect gurgles out the 'happiness' which is called *sāttvik happiness.*'	The *rājasik* 'happiness' arises only when the sense-organs are directly in contact with the sense-object. In the beginning it is quite nectarine and alluring, but it creates in the enjoyer a sense of exhaustion and dissipastion in the long run. Even when one expriences the *rājasik* type of 'happiness' brought about by the sense-organs, it is tainted by an anxiety of diminution and loss of it. Therefore, the temporary 'happiness' provided by the sense-objects is termed as the '*rājasik* happiness.'	The *tāmasik* 'happiness' is the joy which takes us away from our real nature, creates cultural morbidity in our inner life, and gives the intellect a crust of wrong values and false ideals. In the enjoyment of the *tāmasik* 'happiness.', the permanent, ever existing Goal of Life recedes to the back-ground, and this results in seeking simple gratifications at the flesh level. This kind of pursuit incapacitates the intellect to think out correctly the problems *(ālasya)* that face it and to arrive at a right judgement. When the intellect is weak, the mind seeks to compromise with the temptations, heedless of the voice of the higher in us *(pramāda)*. Such a 'happiness' which deludes the soul, both at the beginning and at the end, is classified as *tāmasik*.

In this stanza, we have the description of the dull type of "fortitude," and it is not very difficult to understand it because a substantial majority of us belong to this type. The steadiness-of-purpose with which one does not give up one's dreams and imaginations, fears and agitations, griefs and sorrows, depressions and arrogance, is the *Dhṛti* of the *Tāmasik* type.

The term dream (*Svapna*) is used here to indicate fancied imaginations thrown up by mind that is almost drowned in sleep. To see things which are not there but are delusorily projected by one's own fancy, is called a dream. The dull personalities project upon the world of objects a dream-like value of reality and false joy, and then laboriously strive to gain them.

Fear (*bhaya*):- Such men of delusion will have many a fancied fear of the future, which of course, may never come to pass, but it can efficiently destory the equilibrium and balance, poise and peace in the individual's life. There are many āmong us who have experienced such fears by the hundred in the past. Some fear that they are going to die, but each following day a healthy man wakes up to face the world! Psychologically, they are victims of a fear-complex. And it is interesting to note with what great tenacity these men hug on to such complexes.

Grief, depression and arrogance (Śoka, viṣāda, mada) :- These again are great channels through which human vitality gets dissipated. A man of extreme 'dullness' will constantly keep these three within his bosom and thereby suffer a sense of self-depletion and inner exhaustion. "Grief" (*Śoka*) is, in general, the painful feeling of disappointment at something that has already happened in the *past;* while "depression" (*Viṣāda*) generally reaches our bosom as a result of our despair regarding the future; and "arrogance" (*Mada*) is the sense of lusty conceit with which a foolish man lives his immoral, low life in the present.

One who follows these five values of life is called by *Kṛṣṇa* a fool (*Durmedhāḥ*), and the constancy with which such a fool follows his life of dreams and fears, griefs and despondencies, arrogance and passion, is indicated as the *Dhṛti* of the *Tāmasik* type.

"Pleasure also is three-fold according to the predominant guṇa in the individual. Here follows the threefold division of 'pleasure,' which is the effect of action;

सुखं त्विदानीं त्रिविधं श्रृणु मे भरतर्षभ ।
अभ्यासाद्रमते यत्र दुःखान्तं च निगच्छति ।।३६।।

Sukhaṁ tvidānīṁ trividhaṁ śṛṇu me bharatarṣabha,
abhyāsād-ramate yatra duḥkāntaṁ ca nigacchati.

सुखम् *sukham* = pleasure; तु *tu* = indeed; इदानीम् *idānīm* = now; त्रिविधम् *trividham* = threefold; श्रृणु *śṛṇu* = hear; मे *me* = of me; भरतर्षभ *bharatarṣabha* = O Lord of the *Bhārata-s;* अभ्यासात् *abhyāsāt* = from practice; रमते *ramate* = rejoices; यत्र *yatra* = in which; दुःखान्तम् *duḥkāntam* = the end of pain; च *ca* = and; निगच्छति *nigacchati.* = (he) attains to.

36. *And now hear from me, O best among the* Bhāratas, *of the three-fold "pleasure," in which one rejoices by practice, and surely comes to the end-of-pain.*

In the logical thought development in this chapter, hitherto we found the three factors that constitute the "impulse of all actions": (1) the knowledge, (2) the actor and (3) the action. Afterwards, the very motive forces in all activity-which not only propel activity, but intelligently control and direct it-the *Buddhi* and the *Dhṛti* have also been shown severally, in their different types.

Every "actor" acts in his field, guided by his "knowledge," ruled by his "understanding" (*Buddhi*), and maintained by his "fortitude" (*Dhṛti*). The dissection and observation of "work" is now complete since we have understood the "anatomy and physiology" of work. The "Psychology" of work is now being discussed: why does man act? In fact, every living creature acts propelled by the same instinct, namely, the craving for happiness.

With the three constituents of action-namely, "knowledge," "agency" and "action"-helped by the right type of "understanding" (Buddhi) and "fortitude" (Dhṛti), every living creature from the womb to the tomb continues acting in the world. To what purpose? Everyone acts for the same goal of gaining happiness, meaning, a better sense of fulfilment.

And though the goal be thus one and the same (viz., happiness), since different types of constituents go into the make-up of our actions, and since we are so different in the texture of our *understanding* and *fortitude,* the path adopted by each one of us is distinctly different from those adopted by all others. In and through the variety of actions in the universe, all people-the good, the passionate, and the dull-seek their own sense of satisfaction.

Since each of the five component parts that make up an "action" is of the three different types,* it follows that

---

* See all the five charts.

"happiness" that is gained by the different types must also be different in its texture, perfection and completeness. Here follows a description of the three types of "happiness."

***Through practice* (*Abhyāsāt*) :-** Through a familiarity of this complete scheme-of-things within, an individual can, to a large extent, come to diagnose himself and understand the why and the wherefore of all his miseries. He can thus learn to re-adjust and re-evaluate his life and thereby come to end his sorrows totally, or at least, alleviate his sorrows.

The closing line of this stanza, 'in which one delights by long practice and surely comes to the end of his sorrows,' is taken along with the following stanza by some commentators such as *Śrīdhara* and *Madhusūdana* Sarasvatī. Śrī Śaṅkara's commentary finds no such necessity. It will be keeping in the line with the style of discussion adopted by *Kṛṣṇa* so far in this chapter if this stanza is taken as an introductory verse, preparing us for the study of the following three stanzas.

What is *Sattvik* (pure) happiness?

यत्तदग्रे विषमिव परिणामेऽमृतोपमम् ।
तत्सुखं सात्त्विकं प्रोक्तमात्मबुद्धिप्रसादजम् ।।३७।।

Yat-tad-agre viṣam-iva pariṇāme-'mṛto-pamam,
tat-sukhaṁ sāttvikaṁ proktam-ātmabuddhi-prasādajam.

यत् *yat* = which; तत् *tat* = that; अग्रे *agre* = at first; विषम् *viṣam* = poison; इव *eva* = like; परिणामे *pariṇāme* = in the end; अमृत उपमम् amṛta *upamam* = like nectar; तत् *tat* = that; सुखम् *sukham* = pleasure; सात्त्विकम् *sāttvikam* = *sāttvik* प्रोक्तम् *proktam* = is declared (to be); आत्मबुद्धिप्रसादजम् *ātmabuddhi-*

prasādajam. = born of the purity of one's own mind due to Self-realisation.

37. That which is like poison at first, but nectar like in the end, that "pleasure" is declared to be Sāttvik (pure), born of the purity of one's own mind, due to Self realisation.

That "happiness" which, in the beginning, is like poison and very painful, but which, when it works itself out, fulfils itself in a nectarine success, is the enduring "happiness" of the 'good' (*Sāttvik*). In short, "happiness" that arises from constant effort is the "happiness" that can yield us a greater beauty and a larger sense of fulfilment. The flimsy "happiness" that is gained through sense-indulgence and sense-gratification is a joy that is fleeting, and after its onslaught there is a terrific under-current that comes to upset our equilibrium and drag us into the depths of despondency.

The joy arising out of inner self-control and the consequent sense of self-perfection is no cheap gratification. In the beginning its practice is certainly very painful and extremely arduous. But one who has discovered in oneself the necessary courage and heroism to walk the precipitous "Path" of self-purification and inward balance, comes to enjoy the subtlest of happiness and the all-fulfilling sense of inward peace. This "happiness" (*Sukham*), arising out of self-control and self-discipline, is classified here by the Lord as *Sāttvik* "happiness."

Born out of the purity of one's own mind (*Ātma Buddhi Prasāda-jam*):- By carefully living the life of the 'good' (*Sāttvik*) and acting in discplined self-control, as far as possible in the world, maintaining the *Sāttvik* qualities in all their "component parts," one can develop the '*Prasāda*' of one's inner nature. The term '*Prasāda*' is very often misunderstood in ritualistic language.

The peace and tranquillity, the joy and expansion, that the mind and intellect come to experience as a result of their discipline and contemplation are the true "*Prasāda*". The joy arising out of spiritual practices, provided by the integration of the inner nature, is called '*Prasāda*'. the joy arising out of the *Prasāda (Prasāda-jam) is the Sāttvik* "happiness." In short, the sense of fulfilment and the gladness of heart that well up in the bosom of a cultured man, as a result of his balanced and self-disciplined life of high ideals and divine values of life, are the enduring "happiness" of all Men-of-Perfection, of all true men of religion.

What is Rājasik (passionate) happiness?

विषयेन्द्रियसंयोगाद्यत्तदग्रेऽमृतोपमम् ।
परिणामे विषमिव तत्सुखं राजसं स्मृतम्।।३८।।

Viṣayendriya-saṁyogād-yat-tad-agre-'mṛto-pamam,
pariṇāme viṣam-iva tat-sukhaṁ rājasam smṛtam

विषय-इन्द्रिय-संयोगात् *viṣaya-indriya-saṁyogāt* = from the contact of the sense-organs with the objects यत् *yat* = which; तत् *tat* = that; अग्रे *agre* = at first; अमृत-उपमम् *amṛta upamam* = like nectar; परिणामे *pariṇāme* = in the end; विषम् *viṣam* = poison; इव *eva* = like तत् *tat* = that; सुखम् *sukham* = pleasure; राजसम् *rājasam* = *rājasik* स्मृतम् *smṛtam* = is declared.

38. That pleasure which arises from the contact of the sense-organs with the objects, (which is) at first like nectar, (but is) in the end like poison, that is declared to be Rājasik (passionate).

That happiness which arises in our bosom when the appropriate world-of-objects comes in contact with our sense-organs is indeed a thrill that is nectarine in the beginning, but unfortunately, it vanishes as quickly as it comes, dumping the enjoyer into a pit of exhaustion and indeed into a sense of ill-reputed dissipation.

Rājasik "happiness" arises only when the sense-organs are actually in contact with the sense-objects. Unfortunately, this contact cannot be permanently established; for the objects are always variable. And the subjective mind and intellect, the instruments that come in contact with the object, are also variable and changing, the sense-organs cannot afford to embrace the sense-objects at all times with the same appetite, and even if they do so, the very object in the embrace of the sense-organs withers and purifies, raising the stink of death. No man can fully enjoy even the passing glitter of joy the sense organs give him, for even at the moment of enjoyment the joy-possibility in it gets unfortunately tainted by an anxiety that it may leave him. Thus, to a true thinker, the temporary joys of sense-objects are not at all satisfactory, since they bury the enjoyer, ere long, in a tomb of sorrow.

This sort of "happiness" is classified as the Rajasik type of "happiness" and is generally pursued by men of passion.*

What is Tāmasik (dull) happiness?

यदग्रे चानुबन्धे च सुखं मोहनमात्मनः ।
निद्रालस्यप्रमादोत्थं तत्तामसमुदाहृतम् ॥३९॥

* See all the five charts.

Yad-agre cānu-bandhe ca sukhaṁ mohanam-ātmanaḥ,
nidrālasya-pramād-otthaṁ tat-tāmasam-udahṛtam.

यत् *yat* = which; अग्रे *agre* = at first; च *ca* = and; अनुबन्धे *anubandhe* = in its consequence; च *ca* = and; सुखम् *sukham* = pleasure; मोहनम् *mohanam* = delusive; आत्मन: *atmanaḥ* = like निद्रा- Nidrā- deep sleep, आलस्य - Alasya- indolence प्रमाद - Pramād - heedlessness, उत्थम् - uttham - arising तत् *tat* = that; सुखम् *sukham* = pleasure; राजसम् *rājasam* = *rājasik* स्मृतम् *smṛtam* = is declared.

39. The pleasure, which at first, and in the sequel, deludes the Self, arising from sleep, indolence and heedlessness, is declared to be Tāmasik (dull).

The "happiness" of the 'dull' (*Tāmasik*) is that which deludes the Higher in us, and vitiates the culture in us; and, when the pursuit of such "happiness" is continued for a length of time, it gives to the intellect a thick crust of wrong values and false ideals, and ruins the spiritual sensitivity of the personality.

This type of *Tāmasik* "happiness" satisfies mere sense-cravings; for such *Tāmasik* "happiness" arises, according to the Lord, from sleep (*Nidrā*), indolence (*Ālasya*) and heedless-ness (*Pramāda*).

Sleep (*Nidrā*) :- It is not the psychological condition of the everyday sleep that is meant here. Philosophically, the term "sleep" stands for "the non-apprehension of Reality,"* and the incapacity of the dull-witted to perceive any permanent, ever-existing goal of life. This encourages one to seek simple sense-gratifications at the flesh level.

---

* Refer *Svāmījīś* discourses on *Māṇḍūkya-Kārikā,* Chapter IV.

Indolence ***(Ālasya)*** **:-** It is the incapacity of the intellect to think out correctly the problems that face it and come to a correct judgement. Such an inertia of the intellect makes it insensitive to the inspiring song of life, and a person having such an intellect is generally tossed here and there by the passing tides of his own instincts and impulses.

Heedlessness **(*Pramāda*) :-** As every challenge reaches us and demands our response to it, no doubt, the Higher in us truly guides our activities; but the lower, indolent mind seeks a compromise and tries to act, heedless of the voice of the Higher. When an individual has thus lived for some time carelessly ignoring the Voice of the Higher, he becomes more and more removed from his divine perfections. He sinks lower and lower into his animal nature.

When such an individual, who is heedless of the higher calls, indolent at his intellectual level and completely asleep to the existence and the play of Reality, seeks "happiness," he only seeks a "happiness" that deludes the soul, both at the beginning and at the end. Such "happiness" is here classified by *Kṛṣṇa* as "dull" (*Tāmasik*).

Here follows a stanza which concludes the subject of our present discussion:

न तदस्ति पृथिव्यां वा दिवि देवेषु वा पुनः ।
सत्त्वं प्रकृतिजैर्मुक्तं यदेभिः स्यात्त्रिभिर्गुणैः ॥४०॥

Na tad-asti pṛthivyāṁ vā divi deveṣu vā punaḥ,
sattvaṁ prakṛtijair-ṁuktam yadebhiḥ syāt-tribhir-guṇaiḥ.

न *na* = not; तत् *tat* = that; अस्ति *asti* = is; पृथिव्याम् *pṛthivyām* = on the earth; वा *vā* = or; दिवि *divi* = in the heavens; देवेषु *deveṣu* = amoung the *deva-s* (gods); वा *vā* = or; पुनः *punaḥ* = again; सत्त्वम् *sattvam* = being; प्रकृतिजैः *prakṛtijaiḥ* = born of *prakṛti* (matter); मुक्तम् *muktam* = freed; यत् *yat* = which; एभिः *ebhiḥ* = form these; स्यात् *syāt* = may be; त्रिभिः *tribhiḥ* = from three; गुणैः *guṇaih.* = by qualities.

40. There is no being on earth. or again in the heavens among the "Deva-" (heavenly beings). who is totally liberated from the three qualities, born of Prakṛti *(matter).*

With the above stanza the exhaustive description of the three *Guṇa-s* as impinging upon the personality of all living organisms, is concluded. On the whole, this section of the chapter has given us a psychological explanation for the variety of men that we meet with, in the world-of-plurality, not only in their personality-structures but also in their individual behaviours. The three types of beings have been described exhaustively-by an analysis of "knowledge," "action," "agent" "understanding and "fortitude." This is only for our guidance so that we know where we stand in our own inner nature and outer manifestations.

If we detect, with the above-mentioned slide-rule of personality, that we belong to the *Tāmasik* or the *Rājasik* types, we, as seekers of cultural expression and growth, are to take warning and strive to heave ourselves into the *Sāttvik* state. Remember, and I repeat, remember, these classifications are given *not to classify others* to provide us with a ready-reckoner to help us in our constant and daily *self-analysis and self-discipline.*

These three *guṇa-s* have been described because there is no living organism in the world, *"no creature either on earth or again among the Gods in heaven,"* who is totally free from the influence of these three *guṇa-s;* no living creature can act or work beyond the frontiers provided by these three *guṇa-s.* Nature (*Prakṛti.*) itself is constituted of these *guṇa-s*; the play of these three *guṇas* is the very expression of *Prakṛti.*

But at the same time, no two creatures react to the world outside in the same fashion, because the proportion in which these three *guṇa-s* come to influence each one is different at different times. These three *guṇa-s* put together are the manifestation of "*māyā.*"* Individuals differ from one another because of the different textures of the *guṇa-s* that predominantly rule over them; it is this *māyā* that gives them their individuality. An individual cannot, at any time, exist without all these three *guṇa-s* whatever be their relative proportion.

No sample of "cofee"* is possible without its three ingredients, the decoction, the milk, and the sugar; but at the same time, the proportion in which they are mixed together may be different from cup to cup, according to the taste of the partaker. He who has transcended the three *guṇa-s* comes to experience the very plurality in the world as the play of the One Infinite. So, let us introspect and evaluate ourselves every day, every minute. Let us avoid

---

* See *Svāmījī's* Discourses on *Kenopaniṣad,* Appendix I : 'Rise and Fall of Man.'

* As enjoyed in Indian homes.

the lower *guṇa-s* and steadily work ourselves up towards the achievement of the *Sāttvik* state. Only after reaching the status of the good (*Sāttvik*) can we be ushered into the State of Godhood-Perfection Absolute.

With these three measuring rods-the qualities (*guṇas*) *Kṛṣṇa* classifies the entire community of man under three distinct types. The criterion of this classification is the texture of man's inner equipments which he brings into play for his achievements in his fields of activity. Accordingly, the *Hindu* scriptures have brought the entire humanity under a four-fold calssification. So, its applicability is not merely confined to India-*but universal.*

Certain well-defined characteristics determine the types of these four classes of human beings; they are not always determined by heredity, or accident of birth. They are termed, in our society, as: the *Brāhmaṇa-s*-with a major portion of *Sattva.* a little *Rajas* and with minimum *Tamas;* the *Kṣatriya*-s-mostly *Rajas* with some *Sattva,* and a dash of *Tamas;* the *Vaiśya-s*-with more *Rajas,* less *Sattva* and some *Tamas;* and the *Śūdra*-s-mostly *Tamas,* a little *Rajas,* with only a suspicion of *Sattva.*

THE FOUR VARṆA-S

Guṇa	*Brāhmaṇa*	*Kṣatriya*	*Vaiśya*	*Śūdra*
Sattva	80%	15%	5%	5%
Rajas	15%	80%	80%	5%
Tamas	5%	5%	15%	90%

This four-fold classification is universal and for all times. Even today it holds good. In modern language, the four type of people may be called: (1) the creative thinkers; (2) the politicians; (3) the commercial employers;

and (4) the labourers (the proletarians). We can easily recognise how each subsequent classification holds in awe and reverence the previous higher class-the employees are afraid of the employer, the commercial men are suspicious of the politicians and the politicians tremble at the courageous, independent thinkers.

In the following stanzas, by the discussions contained in them, in the immediate context of the *Kṛṣṇa-Arjuna* summit talks, the Lord is only trying to make *Arjuna* understand that his inner equipment is such that he can be classified only a *Kṣatriya.* Being *Kṣatriya,* his duty is to fight, championing the cause of the good, and thus establish righteousness. He cannot, with profit, retire to the jungle and meditate for Self-unfoldment, since he will have to grow, first of all, into the status of the *Sāttvik* personality (*Brāhmaṇa*) before he can successfully strive on the path of total retirement and a life of rewarding contemplation. Therefore, with the available texture of mind and intellect, the only spiritual *Sādhanā* left for *Arjuna* is to act vigorously in the field of contention that had reached him unasked. Thereby he can exhaust his existing *vāsanā-s* of *Rajas* and *Tamas.*

In the following verses duties ordained by one's nature (*svabhāva*), and one's station in life (svadharma) are laid out with the thoroughness of a law book:

ब्राह्मणक्षत्रियविशां शूद्राणां च परंतप ।
कर्माणि प्रविभक्तानि स्वभावप्रभवैर्गुणैः ।।४१।।

Brāhmana-kṣatriya-viśām sūdrāṇām ca paraṁtapa,
karmāṇi pravibhaktāni svabhāva-prabhavair-guṇaiḥ.

ब्राह्मण-क्षत्रिय-विशाम् *Brāhmaṇa-kṣatriya-viśām* = of *Brāhmanas-kṣatriya-s* and *Vaiśyas* शूद्राणाम् *śūdrāṇām* = of *sūdra-s*; च *ca* = as also परंतप *paraṁtapa* = *O Paraṁtapa;* कर्माणि *karmāṇi* = duties; प्रविभक्तानि *pravibhaktāni* = are distributed; स्वभावप्रभवैः *svabhāva-prabhavaiḥ* = born of their own nature; गुणैः *guṇaiḥ* = by qualities.

41. *Of scholars (Brāhmaṇa-s) of leaders* (Kṣatriya-s) *and of traders* (Vaiśya-s), *as also of workers* (Śūdra-s), *O Paramtapa, the duties are distributed according to the qualities born of their own nature.*

After dealing with the various *guṇa-s* in the preceding stanza, *Kṛṣṇa* now applies them to the social fabric of humanity and thus intelligently classifies the entire mankind under four distinct heads: the*Brāhmaṇas* the *Kṣatriya-s,* the *Vaiśya-s* and the *Śūdras.*

Different types of duties are assigned to each of these classes of individuals depending upon their nature (*Svabhāva*), which is ordered by the proportion of the *guṇa-s* in the makeup of each type of inner equipment. The duties prescribed for a particular type depend upon the manifestation of the inner ruling *guṇa-s* as expressed in the individual's contact with the world and his activities in society. The good and bad are not diagnosed by merely examining the texture of the person's skin or the colour of his hair; an individual is judged only by his expressions in life and by the quality of his contacts with the world outside. These alone can reflect one's inner personality-the quality and texture of the contents of one's mind-intellect.

After testing and determining the quality of the inner

personality, the individuals in the community are classified, and different types of duties are prescribed for each. Naturally, the duties prescribed for a Brahmaṇa are different from those expected of a Ksatriya and the work of the Vaiśya and the Śūdra should necessarily be different from that of the Brāhmana and the *Kṣatriya.* The *Śāstra* enjoins; duties, by pursuing which the preponderant *Tamas* can be evolved into *Rajas,* which in its turn, can grow to become *Sattva.* And, even then, the seeker must wait for the sublimation of *Sattva,* when alone the final experience of the Infinite is gained.

By observing a person* one can conclude as to which class he belongs to-whether to the *Brāhmāṇa,* the *Kṣatriya,* the *Vaiśya* or the *Śūdra.* In this context, when we say a man is *Sāttvik,* it only means that the *Sāttvik* qualities are predominant in him; even in the most *Sāttvik* of persons, at times, the *Rājasik* and the *Tāmasik* qualities can and will show up; so too, even in the most *Tāmasik* man, *Sattva* and *Rajas* will necessarily show up sometimes. No one is exclusively of one *guṇa* alone.

Today, as they are now worked out in India, these four classifications have lost much of their meaning. They siginify merely a hereditary birth-right in the society, a mere physical distinction that divides the society into castes and sub-castes. A true *Brāhmaṇa* is necessarily a highly cultured *Sāttvik* man who can readily control his sense-organs, and with perfect mastery over his mind, can raise himself, through contemplation, to the highest peaks

---

* The type of man's 'action,' the quality of his 'ego', the colour of his 'knowledge,' the texture of his 'understanding,' the temper of his 'fortitude', and the brilliancy of his 'happiness' will determine his *varṇa*

of meditation upon the Infinite. But today's *Brāhmaṇa* is one who is claiming his distinction by birth alone and alas! he gets no reverence, because he has not striven to deserve it.

Answering the four types of nature, as determined by their psychological characteristics, there are four kinds of social living, each having a definite function in society. They are described below:

शमो दमस्तपः शौचं क्षान्तिरार्जवमेव च ।
ज्ञानं विज्ञानमास्तिक्यं ब्रह्मकर्म स्वभावजम् ॥४२॥

Śamo damas-tapaḥ śaucaṁ kṣāntir-ārjavam-eva ca,
jñanaṁ vijñānam-āstikyaṁ brahma-karma svabhāvajam

शमः *śamaḥ* = serenity; दमः *damaḥ* = self-restraint; तपः *tapaḥ* = austerity; शौचम् *śaucam* = purity; क्षान्तिः *kṣāntiḥ* = forgiveness; आर्जवम् *ārjavam* = uprightness; एव *eva* = even; च *ca* = and; ज्ञानम् *jñanam* = knowledge; विज्ञानम् *vijñānam* = realisation; आस्तिक्यम् *āstikyam* = belief in God; ब्रह्मकर्म *Brahmakarma* = (are) the duties of *Brāhmaṇa-s;* स्वभावजम् *svabhāvajam* = born of nature

42. Serenity, self-restraint, austerity, purity, forgiveness and also uprightness, knowledge, realisation, belief in God-are the duties of the Brāhmaṇa-s, born of (their own) nature.

Herein we have a detailed enumeration of the duties of a *Brāhmaṇa* born out of his own predominantly *Sāttvik* nature. Serenity *(Śama),* is one of his duties. *Śama* is controlling the mind from running into the world-of-objects seeking sense-enjoyments. Even if we shut off the world-of-objects by carrying ourserlves away from the tumults and temptations of life into a quiet, lonely place, even there our minds will stride forth into the sense-fields through the memories of our past indulgences. To control consciously this instinctive flow of the mind towards the sense-objects is called *Śama.*

Self-control (Dama) :- Controlling the sense-organs, which are the gateways through which the external world of stimuli infiltrates into our mental domain and mars our peace, is called *Dama.* A man practising *Dama,* even if he be in the midst of sensuous objects, is not disturbed by them. A true *Brāhmaṇa* is one who practises constantly both *Śama* and *Dama,* serenity and self-control.

Austerity (Tapas) :- Conscious physical self-denial in order to economise the expenditure of human energy so lavishly spent in the wrong channels of sense-indulgence and conserving it for reaching the higher unfoldment within is called *Tapas.* By thc practicc of *Śama* and *Dama,* the *Brāhmaṇa* will be steadily controlling both the mad rush of his senses and his mind-wandering. This helps him to conserve his inner vitality which would have been otherwise spent in hunting after sense-joys. This conserved energy is utilised for higher flight in meditation. This subjective process of economising, conserving, and redirecting one's energies within is called Tapas. It is a *Brāhmaṇa's* duty to live in *Tapas.*

Purity (Śaucam) :- Thė *Samskṛta* term used here includes external cleanliness and internal purity. Habits of cleanliness in one's personal life and surroundings are the governing conditions in the life of one who is practising both *Śama* and *Dama.* The practice of *Tapas* makes him such a disciplined person that he cannot stand any disorderly confusion or state of neglect around and about him. A person living in the midst of things thrown about in a disorderly manner is certainly a man of slothful nature and slovenly habits. It is the duty of the *Brāhmaṇa* to keep himself even clean and pure.

Forbearance **(*Kṣāntiḥ*) :-** To be patient and forgiving and thus to live without struggling even against wrongs done against one, is "forbearance"-the duty of a *Brāhmaṇa*, Such an individual will never harbour any hatred for anyone; he lives equanimously amidst both the good and the bad.

Uprightness **(*Ārjavam*) :-** This is a quality which makes an individual straightforward in all his dealings, and his uprightness makes him fearless in life. He is afraid of none, and he makes no compromise of the higher calls with the lower murmurings.

Cultivating the above six qualities-serenity (*Śama*), self-control (*Dama*), austerity (*Tapas*), purity (*Śaucam*), forbearance (*Kṣāntiḥ*), and straight-forwardness (*ārjavam*)- and expressing them in all his relationships with the world outside is the life-long duty of *Brāhmaṇa.* The above mentioned six artistic strokes complete the picture of a *Brāhmaṇa* on the stage of the world when he deals with things and beings in the various situations in life. The Lord enumerates, in the stanza, three more duties of a *Brāhmaṇa* which are the rules of conduct controlling his spiritual life.

Knowledge **(*Jñānam*) :-** The theoretical knowledge of the world, of the structure of the equipments-of-experience and their behaviour while coming in contact with the outer world, of the highest goal of life, of the nature of the spirit-in short, knowledge of all that the

Upaniṣad-s deal with-is included in the term *Jñānam.*

Wisdom (Vijñānam) :- If 'theoretical knowledge' is *Jñānam* then 'personal experience' is *Vijñānam.* Knowledge digested and assimilated brings home to man an inward experience, and thereafter, he comes to live his life guided by this deep inner experience called "wisdom." Knowledge can be imparted, but "wisdom" is to be found by the individual in himself. When a student discovers in himself the enthusisam to live the knowledge gained through his studies, then from the field of his lived experience arises "wisdom"- *Vijñānam.*

Faith (*Āstikyam*) :- Unless one has a deep faith in what one has studied and lived, the living itself will not be enthusiastic and full. This ardency of conviction which is the motive-force behind one who lives what he has understood, is the secret sustaining power that steadily converts Knowledge into "wisdom." This inner order, this intellectual honesty, this subtle unflagging enthusisam, is called "faith."

To grow and steadily cultivate knowledge, wisdom and faith are the sacred duties of a *Brāhmaṇa* in his spiritual life.

What are duties of a *Kṣatriya*?

शौर्यं तेजो धृतिर्दाक्ष्यं युद्धे चाप्यपलायनम् ।
दानमीश्वरभावश्च क्षात्रं कर्म स्वभावजम् ।।४३।।

Śauryaṁ tejo dhṛtir-dākṣyaṁ yuddhe cāpy-apalāyanam,
dānam-īśvara-bhāvaś-ca kṣātraṁ karma svabhāvajam.

शौर्यम् *śauryam* = prowess; तेजः *tejaḥ* = splendour; धृतिः *dhṛtiḥ* = firmness; दाक्ष्यम् *dākṣyam* = dexterity; युद्धे *yuddhe*

= in battle; च *ca* = and; अपि *api* = also; अपलायनम् *apalāyanam* = not flying; दानम् *dānam* = generosity; ईश्वरभावः *īśvara-bhāvaḥ* = lordliness; च *ca* = and; क्षात्रम् *kṣātram* = of *Kṣatriya-s;* कर्म *karma* = action; स्वभावजम् *svabhāvajam* = born of nature

43. Prowess, splendour, firmness, dexterity, and also not fleeing from battle, generousity, lordliness- these are the duties of the Kṣatriya-s, born of (their own) nature.

The *Kṣatriya-s* have a greater dose of *Rajoguṇa* in the composition of their personality. A *Kṣatriya* is not defined by Lord *Kṛṣṇa* as the lawful son of another *Kṣatriya.* He enumerates a series of qualities and behaviours noticed in a truly *Kṣatriya* personality. In the *Gītā*, the four "castes" are described in terms of their manifested individuality when coming in contact with the world-of-objects-the field of expression. In all these descriptions we meet with details of the individual's mental and intellectual reactions to his moral life.

Prowess and Boldness (*Śauryam and Tejaḥ*) :- These mean the vigour and constancy with which he meets the challenges in his life. He who has the above two qualities, heroism and vigour of pursuit. certainly becomes a commanding personality.

***Fortitude* (*Dhṛti*) :-** This is already explained in earlier stanzas. Herein, as applied to a *Kṣatriya*, it is the powerful will of the personality, who, having decided to do something, pursues the "path" and discovers in himself the necessary drive and constancy of purpose to meet, and if necessary breaks down all the obstacles until he gains victory or success.

Promptitude (Dākṣyam):- The *Samskṛta* equivalent for the army parade-ground command "Attention" is "*Dakṣa*!" This quality of alertness and smart vigilance is, indeed, *Dākṣyam.* In the context here, it means that a *Kṣatriya* is prompt in coming to decisions and in executing them. Such an individual is industrious and has an enviable amount of perseverance, however hazardous may the field of his activity be.

Not fleeing from battle:- One who has all the above qualities can never readily accept defeat in any field of conflict. He will not leave any work incomplete, Since *Kṛṣṇa* is here generally classifying all human beings according to the *guṇa-s* predominant in them, these terms should be understood in their greatest amplitude of suggestion. No doubt, a true warrior should not step back in any field of battle; but such literal interpretation is only incomplete. The field-of-battle should include all fields of competition wherein things and situations arrange themselves in opposition to the planned schemes of a man of will and dash. In no such condition will a true *Kṣatriya* feel nervous. He never leaves a field which he has entered; if at all he leaves, he leaves with the crown of success!

Generosity (Dānam) :- Governments or kings cannot be popular unless they loosen their purse-strings. Even in modern days every government budget in all democratic countries has amounts allocated under heads which are not discussed and voted. A man of action cannot afford to be miserly since his success will depend upon his influence on a large number of friends and supporters. The glory of a prince is in his compassion for others who are in need of help.

***Lordliness* (*Īśvara-bhāva*) :-** As a rule, without self-confidence in one's own abilities one cannot lead others. A leader must have such a firm faith in himself that he will be able to reinforce other frail hearts around him with his self confidence. Thus lordliness is one of the essential traits in a *Kṣatriya.* He must waft all around a fragrance of brilliance and dynamism, electrifying the atmosphere around him. A king is not made by his golden robes or be-jewelled crown. The crown, the robe and the throne have a knack of electing for themselves a true wearer. Lordliness is the hallmark of *Kṣatriya.*

These eight qualities-bravery, vigour, constancy, resourcefulness, promptitude, courage in the face of the enemy, generosity and lordliness-are enumerated here as the duties of a *Kṣatriya,* meaning that it is the duty of a true man-of-action to cultivate, to maintain and to express these traits in himself. In no society can leaders of men and affairs claim to be at once the spiritual leaders of the people. Secular heads cannot be spiritual guides. But a true leader is one who has the subtle ability to incorporate the spiritual ideals of our culture into the work-a-day life and maintain them in the community in all its innumberable fields of activity.

*The **duties of the Vaiśya-s and Śūdra-s** are described in the following:*

कृषिगौरक्ष्यवाणिज्यं वैश्यकर्म स्वभावजम् ।
परिचर्यात्मकं कर्म शूद्रस्यापि स्वभावजम् ।।४४।।

Kṛṣi-gaurakṣya-vāṇijyaṁ vaiśya-karma svabhāvajaṁ,
pari-caryātmakaṁ karma śūdrasyāpi svabhāvajam.

कृषि-गौरक्ष्य-वाणिज्यम् *Kṛṣi-gaurakṣya-vāṇijyam* = agriculture, cattle-rearing and trade; वैश्य-कर्म *vaiśya-karma* = the duties of the *Vaiś*ya; स्वभावजम् *svabhāvajam* = born of nature परिचर्यात्मकम् *paricary-ātmakam* = consisting of service of all; कर्म *karma* = action; शूद्रस्य *śūdrasya* = of the *śūdra* अपि *api* = also; स्वभावजम् *svabhāvajam* = born of nature

44. Agriculture, cattle-rearing and trade are the duties of the Vaiśya-s, born of (their own) nature; and service is the duty of the Śūdra-s, born of (their own) nature.

Since each mind-intellect equipment is governed and ruled over by its predominating quality (*guṇa*), each equipment has its own nature to reckon with. A vehicle that can efficiently work in one medium of transport cannot with the same efficiency work in another medium, a car is efficient on the road-but on water? The *Rājasik* mind cannot fly into meditation and maintain its poise as easily and as beautifully as the *Sāttvik* mind can. Similarly, in the field in which a *Kṣatriya* can outshine everybody, a *Vaiśya* or a *Śūdra* cannot. To rise to the highest station in social life, all men cannot have identical opportunities. A social system can only give *"equal opportunities"* to all its members to develop their gifts in and through life. In order to prove this thesis, the various duties are prescribed that will help to mould the personalities of the different types of men.

Agriculture, cattle breeding and tending, trade and commerce are the three fields in which a *Vaiśya* can function inspiredly and exhaust his imperfections. These are duties towards which he has an aptitude because of his own nature. Work in spirit of *dedication and service*

is the duty of a Śūdra.

The mental temperament of a man determines what class he belongs to and each class has been given particular duties to perform in the world. If a man who is fit temperamentally for one type of work is entrusted with a different type of activity, he will bring chaos not only into the field but also in himself. For example, if a *Kṣatriya* were asked to fan someone in a spirit of service, he may condescend to do so, but one will find him ordering somebody else, almost instinctively, to fetch a fan for him! So too, if a man of commercial temperament, a *Vaiśya*, comes to serve as a temple-priest, the sacred place will become, ere long, worse than a trading centre; and again, let him become the head of any government, he will, out of sheer instinct, begin doing profitable "business" from the seat of governmental authority; people call it corruption!!

We must analyse and discover the type of *vāsanās* and temperaments that predominate in each one of us and determine what types of men we are. None belonging to the higher groups has any justification to look down with contempt upon others who are of the lower types. Each one serves the society as best as he can. Each one must work in a spirit of dedication for his own evolution and sense of fulfilment. When each one works thus according to his *vāsanā-s* and fully devotes his attention to his prescribed duties, it is said here that he will develop within himself and attain, in stages, the ultimate Perfection.

When a person works devotedly, in the proper field and in the environment best suited to him, he will be exhausting the existing *vāsanā-s* in him. And when the *vāsanā-s* are reduced he will experience tranquillity and peace within, and it will become possible for him to discover more and more concentration and single-pointed contemplation. With these faculties in him, he can ultimately reach the state of Perfection: the life in the Self.

How ?

स्वे स्वे कर्मण्यभिरत: संसिद्धिं लभते नर: ।
स्वकर्मनिरत: सिद्धिं यथा विन्दति तच्छृणु ।।४५।।

Sve sve karmaṇya-bhirataḥ saṁsiddhiṁ labhate naraḥ,
svakarma-nirataḥ siddhiṁ yathā vindati tac-chṛṇu.

स्वे *sve* = in one's own; स्वे *sve* = in one's own; कर्मणि *karmaṇi* = to duty; अभिरत: *a-bhirataḥ* = devoted संसिद्धिम् *saṁsiddhim* = perfection; लभते *labhate* = attains नर: *naraḥ* = man; स्वकर्मनिरत: *svakarma-nirataḥ* = engaged in his own duty; सिद्धिम् *siddhim* = perfection; यथा *yathā* = how; विन्दति *vindati* = finds; तत् *tat* = that; श्रृणु *śṛṇu.* = listen

45. *Devoted, each to his own duty, man attains Perfection. How, engaged in his own duty, he attains Perfection,----listen.*

Each devoted to his own duty, man attains perfection:- By being loyal to our own level of feelings and ideas, to our own development of consciousness, we can evolve into higher states of self-unfoldment.

The truth of this classification of mankind may not be very obvious, if we observe it only superficially. But the biographies of all great men of action declare repeatedly the precision with which this law-of-life works itself out in human affairs. A tiny Corsican boy who was asked to tend sheep refused to do so and reached Paris to become one of the greatest generals the world had ever seen-Napoleon. A Goldsmith or a Keats would rather compose his metres in a garret than take up a commercial job, courting prosperity and a life of comfort. Each one is ordered by his own *Svabhāva*, and each can discover his fulfilment only in that self-ordered field of activity.

By thus working in the field ordered by one's own *vāsanā-s*, if one can live surrendering one's ego and ego-centric desires to enjoy the fruits, one can achieve a sense of fulfilment; and a great peace will arise out of the exhaustion of one's *vāsanā-s.* The renunciation of the ego and its desires can never be accomplished unless there is a spirit of dedication and a total surrender to the Infinite. When unbroken awareness of the Lord becomes a constant habit of the mind, dedication becomes effective and man's evolution starts.

Such an intelligent classification of human beings on the basis of their physical behaviour, psychological structure and intellectual aptitude is applicable not in India only. As Gerald Heard said: "The Āryan-Samskṛti sociological thought, which first defined and named its fourfold structure of society, is as much ours as India's." This four-fold classification is Universal, both in its application in life and its implication in the cultural development of man.

How can one, devoted to ones own duty, attain perfection? "That do thou hear," says Lord Kṛṣṇa -

यतः प्रवृत्तिर्भूतानां येन सर्वमिदं ततम् ।
स्वकर्मणा तमभ्यर्च्य सिद्धिं विन्दति मानवः ।।४६।।

Yataḥ pravṛttir-bhūtānāṁ yena sarvam-idam tatam,
svakarmaṇā tam-abhyarcya siddhiṁ vindati mānavaḥ

यत: *yataḥ* = from whom; प्रवृत्ति: *pravṛttiḥ* = (is) the evolution; भूतानाम् - *bhūtānām* - of beings; येन *yena* = by whom; सर्वम् *sarvam* = all; इदम् *idam* = this; ततम् *tatam* = is pervaded; स्वकर्मणा *svakarmaṇā* = with his own duty; तम् *tam* = him; अभ्यर्च्य *abhyarcya* = worshipping; सिद्धिम् *siddhim* = perfection; विन्दति *vindati* = attains; मानव: *mānavaḥ* = man.

46. From Whom is the evolution of all beings, by Whom all this is pervaded, worshipping Him with one's own duty, man attains Perfection.

In this chapter the four-fold classification of men and the duties of the individuals belonging to each classification are given. When a man acts according to his "nature" (*Svabhāva*) and station-in-life (*Svadharma*), his *vāsanā-s* get exhuasted. This exhaustion of the load of *vāsanā-s* and the consequent sense of joy and relief can be gained only when he learns to work and achieve in a spirit of total self-surrender.

By constantly remembering the higher goal towards which we are working out our way, if we do our work efficiently, this *vāsanā*-exhaustion takes place. The goal to be constantly remembered is indicated in this stanza: "*He from Whom all beings arise and by Whom all this is pervaded.*" The three equipments-the body, the mind and the intellect, that flutter out into activity, are all in themselves inert *matter* with no consciousness in themselves. It is only at the touch of the Light-of-Life that inert *matter* starts singing its *vāsanā-s* through the various activities.

To remember constantly, this Consciousness, the Atman that lends, as it were, dynamism to the matter that invests it in its activities-is to stand apart from all agitations in the field of strife. Just as a musician, constantly conscious of the background drone, sings his songs easily in tune, just as a dancer dances effortlessly to the rhythm of the drum, such a man is never caught on the worng foot ever in life. A new glow of tranquil peace and dynamic love comes to shine through all his actions, and his achievements radiate the shadowless Light-of-Perfection, unearthly and Divine.

Work can thus be changed into worship by attuning our minds all through our activity to the consciousness of the Self. A self-dedicated man so working in the consciousness of the Supreme pays the greatest homage to his Creator. This subtle change in attitude tranforms the shape of even the most dreary situation. Even the most dreadfully unpleasant field of activity is converted into a sacred chamber of devotion-into a silent hall of prayer-into a quiet seat of meditation!

By thus setting one's hands and feet to work in the field-of-objects with one's mind and intellect held constantly conscious of the Divine Presence, one can attain "through the performance of one's own duties, the highest perfection." Work results in self-fulfilment, apart from its legitimate "fruits." The inner personality gets integrated, and such an integrated person grows in his meditation and evolves quickly.

"And yet, why not I go and meditate?---seems to be the honest doubt in Arjuna's *mind.* Kṛṣṇa *answers:*

श्रेयान्स्वधर्मो विगुणः परधर्मात्स्वनुष्ठितात् ।
स्वभावनियतं कर्म कुर्वन्नाप्नोति किल्बिषम् ।।४७।।

Śreyān-svadharmo viguṇaḥ paradharmāt-svanuṣṭhitāt,
svabhāva-niyataṁ karma kurvann-āpnoti kilbiṣam

श्रेयान् *śreyān* = better; स्वधर्मः *svadharmaḥ* = one's own duty; विगुणः *viguṇaḥ* = (though) destitute of merits; पर-धर्मात् *paradharmāt* = then the duty of another; स्वनुष्ठितात् *svanuṣṭhitāt* = (than) the well performed; स्वभाव-नियतम् *svabhāva-niyatam* = ordained by his own nature; कर्म *karma* = actions; कुर्वन् *kurvan* = doing; न *na* = not; आप्नोति *āpnoti* = (he) incurs; किल्बिषम् *kilbiṣam* = sin.;

47. Better is one's own duty (though) destitute of merits, than the duty of another well-performed. He who does the duty ordained by his own nature incurs no sin.

The opening line of this stanza has been exhaustively discussed earlier (III-35). To work in any field ordered by one's own *vāsanā-s* is better, because in that case, there is a chance for exhausting the existing *vāsanā-s.* When an individual strives in a field contrary to the existing *vāsanā-s,* he not only fails to gain any exhaustion of the existing *vāsanā-s,* but also creates a new load of *vāsanā-s,* in his temperament. Hence, it is said here: *"Better is one's own dharma though imperfect than the dharma of another well-performed."*

By performing "duties ordained by one's own nature" (*Svabhāva-Niyatam-Karma*) the individual comes to no evil-meaning, the individual has no chance of imprinting any new impressions on his mind-the impressions which, in their maturity, might force him to strive, to seek, to achieve and to indulge.

This closing chapter of the *Gītā* is a peroration of the beautiful discourse of the inspired Divine, and it is, naturally therefore, a summary of the whole *Gītā.* Hence, we find here a reiteration of almost all the salient ideas which have been discussed earlier, and which are very important for the cure of the "Arjuna-disease.*

Very many students find it difficult to accept this idea readily. They feel that a ready ideal pattern must be insisted upon with a totalitarian force of vehemence upon the entire society, and that the community must be herded into a disciplined, choiceless, dead, geometrical design. Unfortunately, man is dynamically mobile and, in his surging onrush, the irresistible flood of his ideas and ideals will shatter the pattern, even if death and disaster were to befall him. The nature within and without is a mighty power.

And yet, the doubters would come to feel, perhaps, the logic of it* if they consider the following:

(1) the corroding poison in the fangs of a serpent never kills the serpent;

(2) living organisms crawling in fermented wine never get drunk;

(3) the malarial germs in the mosquitoes do not attack them with shivering fevers.

Thus *svabhāva* of each one cannot destory him! If the poison is drawn from the fangs and wine is poisoned, the crawling organisms die. Similarly, if the *Kṣatriya-s* were to perform the duties prescribed for the *Brāhmaṇa*-type of equipment, they would be only doing harakiri. Arjuna was a *Kṣatriya* ; hence retiring from the battle-

---

* See 'Introduction' to *Gītā* in Chapter I.

* The logic behind the assertion in the stanza is that by performing one's own duties ordained by one's own nature, the individual comes to no evil.

field to a jungle for meditation would have destroyed him.

In short, it is no use employing our minds in fields which are contrary to our nature. Everyone has a precise place in the scheme of created things. Each one has his own importance and none is to be despised, for, each can do something which the others cannot do so well. There is no redundancy in the Lord's Creation; not even a single blade of grass, anywhere, at any time, is unnecessarily created! Everything has a purpose. Not only the good but even the bad are also His manifestations and serve His purpose. The *Pāṇḍava-s'* glory, no doubt is great, but the manifestation of the wickedness in the *Kaurava-s* is also the glory of His Creation. Without the latter, the history of the former would not have been complete. Nothing is to be condemned; none to be despised. Every thing is He, And He alone is.

But the duty to which we are bound is, in case, riddled with evil, are we to follow it?---Kṛṣṇa *answers:*

सहजं कर्म कौन्तेय सदोषमपि न त्यजेत् ।
सर्वारम्भा हि दोषेण धूमेनाग्निरिवावृता:।।४८।।

Sahajaṁ karma kaunteya sadoṣamapi na tyajet.
sarvārambhā hi doṣeṇa dhūmenāgnir-ivāvṛtāḥ

सहजम् *sahajam* = which is inborn; कर्म *karma* = actions; कौन्तेय *kaunteya* = O *kaunteya* (lit. O! Son of *Kuntī*); सदोषम् *sadoṣam* = with fault; अपि *api* = even; न *na* = not; त्यजेत् *tyajet* = one should abandon; सर्वारम्भा: *sarvārmbhāḥ* = all undertakings; हि *hi* = for; दोषेण *doṣeṇa* = by evil; धूमेन *dhūmena* = by smoke; अग्नि: *agniḥ* = fire; इव *iva* = like; आवृता: *āvṛtāḥ* = are enveloped, covered.

48. One should not abandon, O Kaunteya, *the duty to which one is born, though faulty; for, are not all undertakings enveloped by evil, as fire by smoke ?*

After explaining this much about the nature (*Svabhāva*) and the corresponding station-in-life (*Svadharma*), *Kṛṣṇa* builds up the idea to a subtle climax. His advice is general and it is meant for all people, of all times, in all situations. Even when the work so ordinated by the existing *vāsanā-s* (*Sahajam Karma*) is full of evil (*Sadoṣam*), *Kṛṣṇa's* advice is that one should not relinquish it (*Na-Tyajet*).

Superficially reading this declaration in a hurry, one is apt to think that this is not spirituality. But to a careful thinker, the term "born with" (*Sahajam*) solves the riddle. There is an ocean of difference between the meanings of the pharases *"born with"* and *"born into."* *Kṛṣṇa* is saying that one should not renounce actions which are ordered by the evil *vāsanā-s born with* individual. But the Lord has not said that one should pursue the evil action one is born into.

There are two forces that control and guide, define and determine, our actions:

(i) the impulses brought forth by the pressure of the mental temperaments within; and

(ii) the pressure of environments that tickles new temptations in ourselves.

One is to follow faithfully, the subjective *vāsanā-s* even if they be defective. But at the same time, we must courageously renounce all the demands that the objective world makes upon us from without.

The *vāsanā-s* one is *born* with are to be lived through, without ego and desire; while the *vāsanā-s*-creating atmosphere into which one is born should not be allowed to contaminate one's personality. *Kṛṣṇa* is very careful in indicating that a spiritual seeker must constantly strive hard to stand apart from the shackling effects of the enivronments. According to the *Gītā,* man is the master of circumstances. To the extent he comes to assert this mastery, to that extent he is evolved.

In fact, *"all actions (work) are clouded by defects as fire by smoke?"* Here the term used to indicate *"work"* (*Ārambha*) is very important. This *Samskṛta* term *Ārambha* means "beginning." The term was used earlier (XII-16) where also we were asked to *"Renounce the sense of agency in activity."* When there is an ego-centric sense of self-arrogation, the "I-am-the-doer" sense, there is, invariably, creation of new *vāsanā-s* and therefore, it is full of defects (*Doṣa*).

This defect is as unavoidable as the appearance of smoke in fire. The more an oven is ventilated in the atmospheric air, the less smoky becomes the fire burning therein. The more our inner bosom is ventilated with the Consciousness Divine, the less will the ego assert, and therefore, no defects can pollute the actions. If there be an influx of worng *vāsanā-s* within, the earlier we exhaust them through "action"-without any ego or ego-centric desire of enjoying their fruits-the quicker shall the load of existing *vāsanā-s* be lifted from our personality.

What is the benefit of thus acting according to the temperaments with which one is born?

असक्तबुद्धिः सर्वत्र जितात्मा विगतस्पृहः।
नैष्कर्म्यसिद्धिं परमां संन्यासेनाधिगच्छति ।।४९।।

Asakta-buddhiḥ sarvatra jitātmā vigata-spṛhaḥ,
naiṣkarmya-siddhiṁ paramāṁ saṁnyāsen-ādhigacchati.

असक्त बुद्धिः *asakta-buddhiḥ* = whose intellect is unattached; सर्वत्र *Sarvatra* = everywhere जितात्मा *jitātmā* = who has subdued his self; विगतस्पृहः *vigata-spṛhaḥ* = whose desires have fled; नैष्कर्म्यसिद्धिम् *naiṣkarmya-siddhim* = the perfection consisting in freedom from action; परमाम् *paramām* = the Supreme; संन्यासेन *saṁnyāsena* = through renunciation; अधिगच्छति *adhigacchati* = (he) attains.

49. He whose intellect is unattached everywhere, who has subdued his self, from whom desire has fled, he, through renunciation, attains the Supreme State of Freedom-from-action.

It must be remembered, that the entire *Gītā* is addressed to Prince Arjuna standing confused at the immensity of his duty. He wants to run away into the jungle and live in a spirit of what he understands as 'renunciation'. Lord *Kṛṣṇa's* thesis in the entire *Gītā* is that a mere running away from life and its duties is not *Saṁnyāsa* nor is it renunciation. Here, in the stanza, the Lord is defining the State-of-Actionlessness (*Naiṣkarmya-Siddhi*). This state is reached when we do not identify ourselves with the equipments-of-*matter* which are the instruments-of-perception, the three instruments of false interpretation of Truth (Body, Mind and Intellect). To regain our life in Pure Consciousness is the Supreme State.

When we forget our spiritual dignity, the misconception of the ego* arises, we lose our real personality and come

* Ego is the perceiver + the feeler + the thinker, who are the product of the past experiences at the body, mind and intellect levels.

to believe that we are merely the limited ego. Such self-forgetfulness can be observed in any drunken reveller. He forgets his individual personality and status in life and assumes to himself a false identity and continues to be in it as long as he is in a state of intoxication. In his false concept of himself the drunken fool acts, disgracing his education and station in life.

The ego arises when we are ignorant and forgetful of our spiritual nature. When this 'ignorance' is ended, threre is the experience of the Infinite Bliss of the All-Full-Consciousness. Naturally, there is no want felt, and therefore, no desire can arise. When desires are absent, the thought-breedings end. When thoughts are dried up, actions which are the parade of thoughts marching out through the archway of the body, are no more. This state is called "actionlessness"-*Naiṣkarmya Siddhi.*

The Supreme State described so elaborately in the *Upaniṣadic* literature and indicated here by the technical term '*Naiṣkarmya-Siddhi*' is that *'wise'* state-of-being wherein there is no 'ignorance.' *Desires* are the children of 'ignorance', *thoughts* arise from desires, actions are thoughts expressed in the outer world. In the spirituo-psychology of *Vedānta,* we may thus say that 'ignorance' is the great-grandfather of action! With the 'knowledge' of the Spirit, 'ignorance' ends, and in that State, thoughts and actions cannot be. This is the State-of-Full-Awakening, and with reference to its previous condition as expressed and manifested through the body, this condition is indicated as *"actionless-ness"* or *"thoughtless-ness"* or *"desireless-ness."*

The *Gītācārya,* in this stanza, declares that this state

of Perfection, defined as the State of Actionless-ness, cannot be gained by a cheap and ignominious escape from the fields of life's activities. Making use of the fields, we must gain in purity by getting rid of the existing *vāsanā-s* through selfless activities. Making use of the fields, we must gain in purity by getting rid of the existing *vāsanā-s,* through selfless activities which are prescribed to each one of us according to the type to which we naturally belong. Arjuna being a "*Kṣatriya,*" his duty is to fight; and by fighting alone will he exhaust his *vāsanā-s.* By the exhaustion of the *vāsanā-s* alone can one hope to reach the Supreme State of Pure Awareness.

An intellect unattached everywhere *(Asakta-Buddhiḥ Sarvatra)* :- An intellect that is attached to sensuous things of the world outside knows no peace within itslef. It gets agitated and the frail body gets shattered as the fuming mind escapes through it, in its hunt for satisfaction among the sense-objects. A 'clean-shaven intellect,'* devoid of all the cobwebs of attachments with the equipments of perception, feeling and thinking, and their respective objects perceived, felt or thought of, is the vehicle that stands dissolved, revealing that which pulsates through them all. This is the true State-of-Actionless-ness and a man who has earlier disciplined his intellect alone can attain it.

In the case of Arjuna, his tall talks of detachment and renunciation were false of escapism paraded as an angelic

---

* Hence the symbolism of clean shaven head in *saṁnyāsa.* This is also the symbolism in keeping a tuft on the crown of the head *(upanayana)* before a *brāhmaṇa* boy is taken near a teacher: the *Brahmacārī* has snapped off all his attachments and maintains only single faithful attachment to the Supreme.

urge. His *Saṁnyāsa* arose out of his "attachment" to his kith and kin, while true *Saṁnyāsa* must arise out of "detachment."

'One who has subdued his ego' (*Jitātmā*):- An intellect of complete detachment is an impossible dream. The seeker subdues his heart which ever seeks its flickering joys in sense gratifications. This self-mastery of the mind is impossible as long as there are even the minutest traces of desire in him. One from whom all desires have fled (*Vigata-spṛhaḥ*) alone can subdue the mind, and such a seeker alone can accomplish the state of complete detachment of his intellect from the world of sense-objects.

Mind is the seat of all vanities of agency, like "I am the doer" sense (*Kartṛtva-bhāvanā*). The intellect is the seat of all false arrogations that "I-am-the-enjoyer" (*bhoktṛtva-bhāvanā*). These two together make up the ego, and it is fed, nurtured and nourished by its clinging attachments (*spṛhā*) to the joy that is in the objects of the world outside. By correct analysis and investigations, when the "*spṛhā*" is dried up, both the *senses of enjoyership and doership* will get steadily sublimated, leaving behind the Infinite experience of the self. The *Gītā* is never tired of repeating that self-restraint and freedom from desire are the unavoidable pre-requisites for spiritual growth. Herein, we have a beautiful example of explaining the Supreme Goal, not in achieving any Higher State, but as the state of complete detachment from the lower urges.

Freedom from action is a condition in which alone can the experience of the Supreme Being rush in...How?...Learn from Me in brief.

सिद्धिं प्राप्तो यथा ब्रह्म तथाप्नोति निबोध मे।
समासेनैव कौन्तेय निष्ठा ज्ञानस्य या परा ।।५०।।

Siddhim prāpto yathā brahma tathā-pnoti nibodha me,
samāse-naiva kaunteya niṣṭhā jñānasya yā parā

सिद्धिम् *siddhim* = perfection; प्राप्तः *prāptaḥ* = attained; यथा *yathā* = as; ब्रह्म *brahma* = brahman (the Eternal); तथा *tathā* = that; आप्नोति *āpnoti* = obtains निबोध *nibodha* = learn; मे *me* = from Me; समासेन *samāsena* = in brief; एव *eva* = even; कौन्तेय *O kaunteya* = *O kaunteya;* निष्ठा *niṣṭhā* = consummation, state: ज्ञानस्य *jñānasya* = of knowledge; या *yā* = or; परा *parā* = highest.

50, How he, who has attained perfection, reaches Brahman (the Eternal), in brief do learn from Me, O!Kaunteya, *that Supreme State-of-Knowledge.*

Here we are told how to get detached from the wrong tendencies in life, and how, to that extent, we attain serenity and composure. Detachment from matter-hallucinations itself is the rediscovery of the spiritual beauty. The following few stanzas make a beautiful section of this chapter which refreshingly reminds us of the various descriptions of a Man-of-Perfection that were given earlier, throughout the Lord's Song. When we thus get purified, meaning, when the intellect becomes free from its attachments, and the mind and body come well under the control of the intellect, then alone are we fit for the "Path-of-Meditation", which is the Process of accomplishing and fulfilling renunciation of the lower, base, ego-sense.

It is not possible to renounce all attachments

completely, unless one experiences the Truth, and thereby becomes the Infinite Self. Our attempt now is to reduce our attachments to the irreducible minimum, leaving but the thinnest film of 'ignorance' veiling the Supreme. *Kṛṣṇa* says here, "*Learn that from Me in brief,** O, son of *Kuntī*, how to remove this last lingering film of 'ignorance' and thereby get permanently established in that Supreme God-consciousness, which is the Self."

The technique-of-meditation *is being described now, this and the following two stanzas explain what should be the condition of the equipments of perception, feeling, and thinking at the time of perfect meditation:*

बुद्ध्या विशुद्धया युक्तो धृत्यात्मानं नियम्य च।
शब्दादीन्विषायांस्त्यक्त्वा रागद्वेषौ व्युदस्य च ।।५१।।

Buddhyā viśuddhayā yukto dhṛtyāt-mānaṁ niyamya ca,
śabdāīn-viṣayāms-tyaktvā rāga-dveṣau vyudasya ca.

बुद्ध्या *buddhyā* = with an intellect; विशुद्धया *viśuddhayā* = pure; युक्तः *yuktaḥ* = endowed with; धृत्या *dhṛtyā* = by firmness; आत्मानम् *ātmānam* = the self; नियम्य *niyamya* = controlling च *ca* = and; शब्दादीन् *śabddīn* = sound and other; विषयान् *viṣayān* = sense objects; त्यक्त्वा *tyaktvā* = reliquishing; रागद्वेषौ *rāga-dveṣau* = attraction and hatred; व्युदस्य *vyudasya* = abandoning; च *ca* = and;

51. *Endowed with a pure intellect; controlling the self by firmness; relinquishing sound and other objects; and abandoning attraction and hatred;....*

---

* The Lord promises here that He is going to explain this aspect of Self-knowledge *(adhyātma vidyā)* in brief, because this technique of meditation for the final release was exhaustivel explained earlier in Chapter V and VI.

**** Endowed with Pure understanding (Viśuddhayā):-*** An intellect that has grown to remain without *vāsanā-s.* An intellect that has thus purified itself of all its tendencies of joy-hunting is indicated here as pure understanding.

**** Controlling the mind and the senses with fortitude:-*** These two sabotage the harmony and balance in a meditator when he is at his seat of meditation. At the moment the sense organs receive a rush of stimuli with which they can disturb the music of meditation in the mind; or, often the mind can topple down from its steady concentration, by itself remembering its own experiences of the past. By controlling both these, which were earlier described as *Śama* and *Dama,* the seeker comes to tune himself up properly. He becomes invulnerable to all such attacks.

The idea of controlling the mind and sense-organs described in the earlier epithet is clearly elucidated in the second line of the stanza.

Renouncing sense-objects :- Controlling the sense-organs means allowing none of the stimuli such as sound, form, touch, taste or smell to infiltrate through their respective gateways of ears, eyes, skin, tongue and the nose. When thus a complete wall-of-understanding has been built around the mind, protecting it from any onslaught from the outer world, the mind can, of its own accord, either dance in some remembered joy, or sob in grief at some expected sorrow-because of its likes and dislikes, loves and hatreds. Therefore, these instinctive impulses of the mind are also to be controlled.

To summarise, a meditator is one who has:

(1) an intellect purified of all its extrovert desires;
(2) a mind, together with the sense-organs, brought well under the control of this intellect, so purified;
(3) the sense-organs no more contacting the sense objects; and
(4) a mind that has given up its ideas of likes and dislikes.

It is this individual who becomes a successful meditator.

Again :

विविक्तसेवी लघ्वाशी यतवाक्कायमानसः।
ध्यानयोगपरो नित्यं वैराग्यं समुपाश्रितः ॥५२॥

Vivikta-sevī laghvāśī yata-vāk-kāya-mānasaḥ,
dhyāna-yoga-paro nityaṁ vairāgyam sam-upāśritaḥ

विविक्त-सेवी *vivikta-sevī* = dwelling in solitude; लघ्वाशी *laghvāśī* = eating but little; यत वाक् काय मानसः *yata-vāk-kāya-mānasaḥ,* = speech, body and mind subdued; ध्यान-योग-परः *dhyāna-yoga-paraḥ* = engaged in meditation and concentration; नित्यम् *nityam* = always; वैराग्यम् *vairāgyam* = dispassion; समुपाश्रितः *sam-upāśritaḥ* = taking refuge in.

52.. Dwelling in solitude; eating but little; speech, body and mind subdued; always engaged in meditation and concentration; taking refuge in dispassion;....

Dwelling in solitude (Vivikta-Sevī) :- A seeker who has developed all the above-mentioned physical, mental and intellectual adjustments, must now seek a sequestered spot of loneliness. This does not mean that he must move out of a town to a jungle. The term indicates only a spot "wherein there is the least disturbance." Even in the midst of a market there are moments when it is deserted and quiet. If the seeker is sincere, he can discover such moments of complete solitude under his own roof.

Eating but little :- Over-indulgence and stuffing oneself with highly nutritive food is fattening the body and thickening the subtlety of one's intellectual activities. Temperance is the law for all spiritual students (VI-17)

Controlling speech, body and mind:- The mind cannot be subdued unless the body is brought under its command. The body is constituted of the sense-organs of perception and action. The grossest manifestation of the mind is action, and to control action is to discipline the mind. The term speech used here indicates "all sense-organs-of-action and their functions", and the term body represents "the organs-of-perception and all their activities of perceiving their respective objects." Unless these two sets of organs are controlled, the mind cannot be subdued.

In fact the *mind itself,* at the body-level, becomes the sense-organs, and the mind projected away from the body is the great universe of sense-objects. When the mind, playing through the body, identifies itself with its own projections-the objects-it is called *perception*; and when it comes in contact with the world-of-objects seeking satisfaction and entertainment, it is called *action.* Disciplining action and regulating perception-in short, eliminating the ego-centric attitude in all our perceptions, in all our relationships with the world-of-objects, is what is advised here.

Ever engaged in meditation : Controlling the actions and perceptions of the mind is not possible as long as the mind is constantly flowing out through the sense-organs towards the sense-objects. Seeking sense-gratifications. the mind is in a constant state of agitation. To quieten such a mind, it is necessary that we must give it some "point-of-contemplation" wherein, as it engages itself more and more, it shall discover consummate happiness and get sufficiently disengaged from everything else. Diverting the mind from the world of sense-objects and maintaining it in a steady flow towards contemplation of the Lord in an utter attitude of identification, is called meditation. To be steadily in a state of such an all-consuming dedication unto a nobler and higher ideal is the method of cooling down the mind's boiling lust for sense enjoyments.

Possessed of dispassion :- Dispassion is *Vairāgya.* It is not a mere self-denial of any object of enchantment, but it is a state when the mind rebounds upon itself from the objects as a result of its discovery that the objects contain no glow of happiness. The essence of dispassion is not in our running away from the objects. From a truly dispassionate man, the objects run away in inexplicable despair.

The principle of supply and demand works also at the personality contacts with the world outside. Towards the drunkard bottles of wine march in, but from a temperate man even the existing bottles in his cupboard march out. Dispassion is necessary, and without it the mind will never grow because growth of the mind will depend upon its capacity to outgrow itself from its present state. At any given moment, the mind's growth is curtailed only by its own world of interests.

When the old interests of a person die away and when

he is ordered by new intellectual visions, new interests rise up in his mind; then the old world-of-objects around him suddenly retires, yielding place to the new set of things that he has willed around him by his newly developed mind. As long as I was a vicious man, sensuous friends and pleasure-seekers crowded my drawing-room; when I changed my way-of-life and took to serious social work and political activities, the group of idlers went away yielding their places to politicians and social workers. After a time I grew in my mental make up, and so, in my spiritual interests, even these politicians with their power-politics, and the social workers with their unspeakable jealousies and rivalries retired, yielding their places to men of thought and spiritual benediction. This is a typical example of how, as a mind grows, it leaves its old toys behind and enters totally into a greater field of the nobler gains of life.

To sum up, a true seeker of the Higher Life must seek solitude, live in temperance, subdue his speech, body and mind, and must live in a spirit of dispassion, a true life of aspiration to heave himself towards the ideal.

These efforts can build up a temple of success only when the inner personality has a deep foundation upon certain enduring values of life. Those are enumerated in the following :

अहंकारं बलं दर्पं कामं क्रोधं परिग्रहम् ।
विमुच्य निर्ममः शान्तो ब्रह्मभूयाय कल्पते ॥५३॥

Ahaṁkāraṁ balaṁ darpaṁ kāmaṁ krodhaṁ parigraham,
vimucya nirmamaḥ śānto brahma-bhūyāya kalpate.

अहंकारम् *ahaṁkāram* = egosim; बलम् *balam* - *power,* दर्पम् *darpam* = *arrongance;* कामम् *kāmam* = desire; क्रोधम् *krodham* = anger; परिग्रहम् *parigraham* = aggrandisement, covetousness; विमुच्य *vimucya* = having abandoned; निर्मम: *nirmamaḥ* = wihtout 'mine'ness; शान्त: *śāntaḥ* = peaceful; ब्रह्म-भूयाय *brahma-bhūyāya* = for becoming *Brahman*; कल्पते *kalpate* = (he) is fit.

53. Having abandoned egoism, power, arrogance, desire, anger and aggrandisement, and freed from the notion of 'mine,' and so peaceful-he is fit to become Brahman.

If the preceding verse indicated things that are to be acquired and brought about in the relatively outer surfaces of the meditator's pesonality, here we have a list of things which are to be renounced from the inner core of the meditator's personality. Here are the enduring values-of-life a meditator must learn to live.

The items enumerated in the stanza are not, in fact, so many different items, but they are all different manifestations of one and the same wrong notion, namely the "I-act-mentality" (*Ahaṁkāra*). When this "sense-of-agency" develops, ego-centric vanities intensify within our bosom, and they manifest as "power" (*Balam*)-the "power" to strive and struggle, sweat and strain, to fulfil passions and desires. A powerful ego will, with each success in the sensuous world, gather to itself more and more "pride," or "arrognace" (*Darpam*).

To an individual personality working under the influence of both "power" and "arrogance," "lust and anger" (*Kāma* and *Krodha*) are but natural, and thereafter, he becomes a mad machine of restlessness within and of disturbances around, ever anxiously bearing himself down upon the society in order that he may, by means fair or foul, acquire, possess and aggrandise the objects of his fancy, indicated here by the term "aggrandisement" (*Parigraha*).

The six items listed above are nothing but manifestations of the "sense-of-agency"-the 'I-act-mentality' (Ahaṁkara). *Kṛṣṇa* asks the meditator to forsake these and thus to immediately become egoless (*Nirmamaḥ*) and peaceful (*Śāntaḥ*). This is not the peace of the grave nor the quiet of the desert; this is the peace that arises out of the fullness of 'wisdom,' out of our absolute satisfaction experienced in the Realm-of-Perfection.

All restlessness is caused by the ego and its onward rush towards finite objects, seeking among the ephemeral, a satisfaction and joy that is permanent and enduring. When this sense-of-agency and endless seeking of sense-gratification have been renounced, the seeker (*sādhaka*) experiences a relative quiet within his bosom. He who is tuned thus, through understanding and discipline, can discover in himself the required balance and equipoise to rocket his total personality into the higher climbs of "conscious unfoldment". The stanza does not say that such an individual has reached Perfection, but it definitely says that *"He is fit to become Brahman."* The above is but a preliminary preparation for the final realisation.

What then is the next stage of development? The *Gītā* explains:

ब्रह्मभूतः प्रसन्नात्मा न शोचति न काङ्क्षति ।
समः सर्वेषु भूतेषु मद्भक्तिं लभते पराम् ।।५४।।

Brahma-bhūtaḥ prasann-ātmā na śocati na kāṅkṣati.
samaḥ sarveṣu bhūteṣu mad-bhaktiṁ labhate parām.

ब्रह्म-भूत: *brahma-bhūtaḥ* = Brahman-become; प्रसन्नात्मा *prasann-ātmā* = serene-minded; न *na* = not; शोचति *śocati* = (he) grieves; न *na* = not; काङ्क्षति *kāṅkṣati* = desires; सम: *samaḥ* = the same; सर्वेषु *sarveṣu* = all; भूतेषु *bhūteṣu* = to beings; मद् भक्तिम् *mad bhaktim* = devotion unto Me; लभते *labhate* = obtains; पराम् *parām* = supreme.

54. Becoming Brahman, *serene in the Self, he neither grieves nor desires; the same to all beings, he obtains a supreme devotion towards Me.*

After liquidating the ego and its manifestations-enumerated in the preceding stanza as power, pride, lust, passion and sense of possession-the seeker comes to experience a relatively greater peace within, as he is released from all the confusions generally created by the psychological mal-adjustments and intellectual false evaluations of life. This newly discovered inner tranquillity, no doubt artificially propped up for the time being by severe self-discipline, should be positively reinforced by definite efforts and constant vigilance.

With constant self-effort, relative peace in the mind is to be maintained for longer periods of time and zealously guarded. Joys and sorrows will be constantly reaching our bosom from the outer world; we are helpless before them. For, even when the "sense-of-agency: has been renounced, the other aspect of the ego, "I-enjoy-mentality" (*Bhoktṛtva-bhāvanā*) will assert itself and poison the mind of the meditator. A worm cut into two pieces becomes two separate, independent living worms ere long. So too, if one aspect of the ego, the "I-do-mentality" is conquered, we must equally attend to the destruction of the other aspect of the ego, the "I-enjoy-mentality"; or else, the surviving part will revive within a very short time and we shall discover a healthier ego, potentially more powerful, dangerously rising out of the seemingly dead individuality.*

One who has read well, reflected upon and understood the theme of the Absolute Reality as discussed in the Scriptures, is indicated here by the term "*Brahma-Bhūtaḥ.*" This word employed in this verse should not be construed as "one who has become Brahman." It can only mean "one who has convinced oneself of the existence and nature of the Reality as discussed in the Scriptures." Once this Spiritual Truth is understood, the student necessarily becomes less agitated, because, all disturbances enter our life through our identification with the equipments-of-experiences only. To the extent an intellect realises the existence of the diviner aspect in it, and so automatically withdraws its all-out clinging to the matter-realm, to that extent it is not disturbed by the objects of perception, feeling and thought. Thus it discovers a growing tranquillity (*Prasannātmā*) within itself.

A seeker who has gained the "knowledge" of *Brahman* through *study*, and made it his own through reflection, gains the tranquillity of composure as a result of his understanding, and therefore experiences a partial liquidation

---

* This is the secret psychology behind such *sādhaka* or monks who, after an initial period of renunciation and divine seeking, suddenly leave their life of self-control or sacred robes and live a sensuous life. The 'I enjoy' mentality of the ego has not been fully transcended by them during '*sādhanā.*'

of his ego-sense. Thereby he discovers in himself the courage to stand apart, both from grief and desire. He grieves not (*Na Śocati*) because he feels no incompleteness in himself, as he used to feel in the earlier days of his arrogant ego. Since there is no sense of imperfection, his intellect no longer spins new and novel plans for satisfactions and temporary gratifications, which are called desires, Naturally, one who grieves not in life desires not (*Na Kāṅkṣati*) for the possession of anything to make his happiness complete.

A tranquil seeker-who, in his understanding, comes to desire nothing and has developed an independent source of happiness which is free from the presence or the absence of any external environment-lives in the world, with a totally new set of values of life, in which, according to him, there is nothing but the constant experience of the Divine Presence. Naturally, he develops an equanimity of vision (Refer V-18, 19 and 20).

This type of an individual attains supreme devotion unto Me:- Earlier, an entire chapter (Ch.XII) has been devoted to the discussion on devotion wherein we found that, according to the Scripture, devotion is measured by our sense of identification with the Higher Ideal. In order to identify with the Infinite Truth, the seeker must have a definite amount of detachment from his usual channels of dissipation, both in the outer world and the realms within.

The previous verse indicated the methods of detachment and it was said that he who accomplished them in his inner composition is the only one who is capable of striving for and succeeding in a true identification with the play of the Infinite in and through the finite. The expansiveness of vision, the catholicity of love and the release from sense preoccupation-all these are necessary in order to produce in the seeker, supreme love for the Lord. There is yet another stage in one's pilgrimage to Truth.

What exactly then is the next stage ?

भक्त्या मामभिजानाति यावान्यश्चास्मि तत्त्वतः ।
ततो मां तत्त्वतो ज्ञात्वा विशते तदनन्तरम् ।।५५।।

Bhaktyā mām-abhijānāti yāvān-yaś-cāsmi tattvataḥ,
tato māṁ tattvato jñātvā viśate tad-anantaram.

भक्त्या *bhaktyā* = by devotion; माम् *mām* = Me; अभिजानाति *abhijānāti* = he knows; यावान् *yāvān* = what; यः *yaḥ* = who; च *ca* = and; अस्मि *asmi* = (I) am; तत्त्वतः *tattvataḥ* = in essence; ततः tataḥ = then; माम् mām = Me; तत्त्वतः tattvataḥ = in Essence; ज्ञात्वा *jñātvā* = having known; विशते *viśate* = (he) enters; तद्-अनन्तरम् *tad-anantaram* = forthwith, at once.

55. By devotion he knows Me in Essence, what and who I am; then, having known Me in My Essence, he forthwith enters into Me-the Supreme.

By devotion he comes to know Me:- Devotion, as we have explained, is "love for the Supreme." Love is measured by the degree of identificaiton the lover maintains with the beloved. When an ego-centric individuality, having made all the above adjustments, increasingly seeks and discovers its identity with the Self, it comes to experience the true nature of the Self more and more clearly. Such a seeker comes to understand *"what and who I am."*

In the entire *Gītā* the first peson singular is used by the Lord to indicate the Supreme Goal. It is not Lord *Kṛṣṇa*, as an individual person who is indicated by the terms 'I' and 'Me' as used in these discourses, Remember, this is the Lord's own Song, sung to revive His devotees, and the pronouns used here represent the *Paramātman.* To know the Self means to know both Its nature and identity. these are the topics in all scriptures. But the scriptural study gives us only an intellectual comprehension of Truth and not its Essence (*Tattvataḥ*), a spiritual apprehension of Truth as a lived experience.

Then having known Me in essence:- When this experience comes through a slow and steady unfoldment of the Light of Consciousness, through the dropping of the veils of 'ignorance' created by our identifications with the body, we come to apprehend, in toto, the Infinite. The individuality or the ego, ends and *"HE THEREATER ENTERS ME."*

The "*entry*" mentioned here is not like that of a man entering a structure-a house which is separate from himself-and he is entering the house where he is not at the moment. There is no ego to enter into the plane of God-consciousness. The term "*entry*" is used here exactly in the same fashion as "the dreamer *enters* the waking state." The dreamer cannot retain his own individuality when he enters the waking but he himself becomes the "waker." Similarly, when the ego *enters* God-consciousness, the individuality cannot retain itself as such. The misconception that he is an individual ends and he rediscovers, becomes or awakens to, the Infinite *Brahman-hood-the State of Kṛṣṇa-Consciousness.*

Devotion for the Lord is never complete without service to the living world of creatures:

सर्वकर्माण्यपि सदा कुर्वाणो मद्व्यपाश्रयः ।
मत्प्रसादादवाप्नोति शाश्वतं पदमव्ययम् ।।५६।।

Sarva-karmāṇy-api sadā kurvāṇo mad-vyapāśrayaḥ.
mat-prasādād-avāpnoti śāśvataṁ padam-avyayam.

सर्व-कर्माणि *sarva-karmāṇi* = all actions; अपि *api* = also; सदा *sadā* = always; कुर्वाणः *kurvāṇaḥ* = doing; मद्-व्यपाश्रयः *mad-vyapāśrayaḥ* = taking refuge in Me; मत्-प्रसादात् *mat-prasādāt* = by My grace; अवाप्नोति *avāpnoti* = obtains; शाश्वतम् *śāśvatam* = the eternal; पदम् *padam* = state of abode; अव्ययम् *avyayam* = indestructible.

56. Doing all actions, always taking refuge in Me, by My grace, he obtains the Eternal, Indestructible State or Abode.

The philosophy of the *Gītā* is extremely dynamic. The Song of the Lord is an innocent-looking magazine of power which can be detonated by correct understanding. The warmth of living makes it explode, blasting the crust of ignorance that has grown around the noble personality and its divine possibilities in the student.

Devotion *(Bhakti)* to the Lord, in the *Gītā,* is not a mere passive surrender unto the ideal, nor a mere physical ritualism. Lord *Kṛṣṇa* insists, not only upon our identification with the Higher through an intelligent process of detachment, from the both the senses, of "*agency*" and "*enjoyment,*" but also upon the understanding and the inner experience positively brought out in all our contacts with the outer world, in all our relationships.

Religion, to Lord *Kṛṣṇa,* is not fulfilled by a mere withdrawal from the outer world of sense objects, but in a definite come-back into the world, bringing into it the fragrance of peace and joy of the yonder, to brighten and beautify the drab, inert objects that constitute the world. Therefore, after describing one who can be considered as the higher devotee, in this stanza, *Kṛṣṇa* now adds another condition to be fulfilled by all seekers.

The *Gītācārya* never wants to receive any devotee at His gate, nor will He give an audience to anyone, unless the seeker carries the passport of selfless service to the society-"*Performing continuously all actions, always taking refuge in me.*"

In order to serve without the "sense-of-agency," the practical method is "take refuge in Me." Such a seeker, who is constantly working in fulfilling his obligatory duties to the society and towards himself has "My grace" (*Matprasāda*).

The Supreme has no existence apart from His Grace; He is His Grace, His Grace is He, the Grace of the Self, therefore, means more and more the play of Divine Consciousness in and through the personality layers in the individual. In an individual, to the extent his mind and intellect are available, in their discipline to be ruled over by spiritual truth, to that extent he is under the blessings of His Grace.

He attains the eternal immutable state:- When thus working in the world, without the 'sense of agency and enjoyment,' the existing *vāsanā-s* become exhausted, the ego gets eliminated. Awakening thus from the delusory projections of the ego, the individual attains the State of Pure Consciousness and comes to live thereafter the Eternal, Immortal State-The *Kṛṣṇa-State-of-Perfection.*

In the preceding three stanzas the "Paths" of Knowledge, Devotion and Action are indicated, and in all of them the same goal of realising the seeker's oneness with the Supreme has been indicated.* Integral *Sādhanā* is the core of the *Gītā* technique. To synthesize the methods of Work, Devotion and Knowledge is at once the discipline of the body, mind, and intellect. For, all disciplines pursued from the body level, in order to control the mind and turn it towards the ideal, are called *Karma Yoga;* all methods of channelising emotions in order to discpline the mind to contemplate upon the Higher are called *Bhakti Yoga,* and all study and reflection, detachment and meditation, practice at the intellectual level, whereby, again the mind is lifted to the realm of the silent experience of its own Infinitude are called *Jñāna Yoga.*

To practise all the three during our life is to discipline all the three layers in us. Thus, the philosophy of total spiritual transformation of the perceiver, the feeler and the thinker, all at once, is the prime contribution that the *Gītā* has to make to the timeless tradition of the *Hindu culture,* as available for us in the *Upaniṣad-s.*

Therefore:

---

1. *Prasāda*--See *Kaṭhopaniṣad,* wherein 'grace' was discussed as the inner purity *(dhātu-prasāda).*
2. Stanza 54--*Madbhaktim labhate parām;*
3. Stanza 55--*Mām viśate tadanantaram;*
   Stanza 56--*Avāpnoti Śāśvatam padam avyayam.*

चेतसा सर्वकर्माणि मयि संन्यस्य मत्परः ।
बुद्धियोगमुपाश्रित्य मच्चित्तः सततं भव ॥५७॥

Cetasā sarva-karmāṇi mayi saṁnyasya mat-paraḥ,
buddhi-yogam-upāśritya mac-cittaḥ satatam bhava.

चेतसा *cetasā* = mentally; सर्व-कर्माणि *sarva-karmāṇi* = all actions; मयि *mayi* = in Me; संन्यस्य *samnyasya* = resigning; मत्-परः *mat-paraḥ* = having Me as the highest goal; बुद्धि-योगम् *buddhi-yogam* = the *Yoga* of discrimination; उपाश्रित्य *upāśritya* = resorting to; मत्-चित्तः *mat-cittaḥ* = with the mind fixed on Me; सततम् *sattatam* = always; भव *bhava = be.*

57. Mentally rencouncing all actions in Me, having Me as the Highest Goal, resorting to the Yoga-of-discrimination, ever fix your mind in Me.

Resigning mentally all actions to me :- Both the ego and the ego-centric anxieties for enjoying are to be rencounced at the alter of the Lord, and thus to act in the world is the 'path,' through which a man of action reaches the greater cultural climes. This idea of surrender has been discussed earlier, very exhaustively.* This spirit of surrender can come only when the student has infinite courage to maintain a steady aspiration for "*Having me as the highest goal.*" The mind needs a positive hold upon something, before it can be persuaded to leave its present props.

Resorting to Buddhi Yoga :- The intellects' main function is discrimination. To discriminate the false from the true, and to fix ourselves on the path of seeking the true, is called *Buddhi Yoga.* Controlling life and regulating

---

* See commentaries on the most crucial stanza in Chapter III--Stanza 30.

its movements through discrimination is *Karma Yoga.* And thus the term 'Buddhi Yoga' is an original coined-word, met with only in the *Gītā,* to indicate in essense the "Path-of-Selfless-Action." It has been used in the very early portions of the *Gītā** and there it has been very exhaustively explained.

Please ever fix your mind on Me :- One who has fixed *Kṛṣṇa-tattva* as the goal of his life, one who surrenders himself mentally at all times at this altar, and serves all His creatures one who ever discriminates and avoids all undivine thoughts and ego-centric self-assertions-such a one alone can naturally come to fix his thoughts constantly upon the Lord.

It is an eternal law of mental life that "as we think so we become." A devotee who has thus come to live all his activities in dedication to his goal, the *Kṛṣṇa*-Consciousness, must necessarily come to live as *Kṛṣṇa,* and experience the Eternal, Immutable, State of the Self.

Suppose one refuses to follow this seemingly arduous 'Path,' what would be his condition?....Listen:

मच्चित्तः सर्वदुर्गाणि मत्प्रसादात्तरिष्यसि ।
अथ चेत्त्वमहंकारान्न श्रोष्यसि विनङ्क्ष्यसि ॥५८॥

Mac-cittaḥ sarva-durgāṇi mat-prasādāt-tariṣyasi,
atha cet-tvam-ahamkārān-na śroṣyasi vinaṅkṣyasi.

मत्-चित्तः *mat-cittaḥ* = fixing your mind on Me; सर्व-दुर्गाणि *sarva-durgāṇi* = all obstacles; मत्-प्रसादात् *mat-prasādāt* = by My grace; तरिष्यसि *tariṣyasi* = (you) shall overcome; अथ *atha* = now चेत् *cet* = if; त्वम् *tvam* = you; अंहकारात्

---

* Refer II-39, wherein we have exhausively described the *Buddhi Yoga.*

ahaṃkārāt = from egoism; न *na* = not; श्रोष्यसि *śroṣyasi* = you will hear; विनङ्क्ष्यसि *vinaṅkṣyasi* = (you) shall perish.

58. Fixing your mind upon Me, you shall, by My grace, overcome all obstacles, but if, from egoism, you will not hear Me, you shall perish,

Though the vigorous personality of Arjuna was under a historical coma at the beginning of the *Gītā*, it has by now revived to feel native thirst of the *Āryan* heart to be practical at all moments. He wants to acquire the perfections indicated in *Kṛṣṇa's* discourses. He is not one who is satisfied with a mere bundle of ideal dreams or fascinating discussion on some possibilities. He wants a practical method to attain the Infinite, and *Kṛṣṇa* gives him the necessary practical tips.

Lord *Kṛṣṇa,* in essence, says: "By your thoughts, renounce all your activities in Me." All activities in the world are only expressions of the Divine Consciousness flashing Its brilliance through the body. In all activities be conscious of the Lord, without Whom no action is ever possible. Keep Him as your Goal. Make your intellect constantly aware of this "Lord of all actions." Gradually, the mind and the body will begin to work under the command of such an inspired intellect.

We make mistakes in life only when our intellect does not function properly in coming to its correct judgements. Often our intellect becomes itself a victim of the the impulses and instincts of our lower nature, the mind. To keep the intellect consciously wakeful, one must always remember the Presence within and perceive without, the Play of the Lord to whom alone all actions belong. A devotee is like an ambassador of a country who constantly remembers, in thought, speech and action, at all the times during his sojourn in the capital to which he has been appointed, that he is a representative of his country. so long as we are in the body, mind and intellect, we have to remember constantly that we are but His 'appointed' agents through whom the Infinite plays.

How will this constant remembrance of the Lord help? This is now being answered. *Kṛṣṇa* says: "He who has completely fixed all his thoughts upon me, will cross over all difficulties by my grace." Most of our obstacles in life are imaginary-created by false fears and deceitful anxieties of our own confused mind. The "grace" referred to here is "the result accrued in our mind when it is properly tuned up to and peacefully settled in contemplation upon the Infinite." It does not mean any special consideration shown by the all loving Lord to some rare persons of His own choice. The Grace of the all-pervading is present everywhere because Grace is His form. Just as the ever-present sunlight on a bright day cannot illumine my room as long as the windows are closed, so too, the harmony and joy of life of the Infinite cannot penetrate into our life, as long as the windows of discrimination in us are tightly shut. To the extent the windows of my room are opened, to that extent the room is flooded by the sunlight; to the extent a seeker puruses his *sādhanā* and brings about the above-mentioned adjustments, to that extent the Grace of the Self shall flood his within.

By constantly remembering the Lord and his glories, cultivate a nobler and higher goal of life. By this process we conserve our personality-energy which, as it is, gets unfortunately dissipated in sense-indulgences, in the hellish streaking stroms of lust, in the sweeping floods of passion, and in the flowing lava of desires, When this unintelligent, and now unnoticed, dissipations are controlled, the human mind re-discovers in itself a new vitality and strength added into its greater potentialities.

In the second line of the verse, the Lord warns against all those who, in their utter ignorance, disobey this Law of Life. Natural laws are irrevocable; they have neither eyes, nor ears. They just continue in their own rhythm and that man is happy who discovers the law and obeys it implicitly.*

***But if, from egoism, you will not hear me, you shall perish* :-** This is not a threat hurled down upon mankind by a tyrannical power, to frighten the human beings into obedience. This is not comparable with the threat of hell held out by other religions. This is a mere statement of fact; even if Newton himself were to jump from the third floor balcony of his house, the gravitational force would indeed, act upon him also! There is an inevitability in nature's laws, Man is free to choose freedom or bondage. The path of freedom is described above, and in this open and sincere statement, the Lord is only showing great anxiety, not to mince matters, but to be callously frank in His expressions.

Guidance to this true "way-of-life" always comes to us from the depth of our nature, expressed in the language

* This statement is often mis-understood by today's hasty generation as the tyrannical laws of religion. A little thought will clear this misunderstanding. If scientific discoveries in the world have brought the natural forces under man's service, it is only because science has discovered the laws that govern them, and the generation has condescended to follow implicitly these laws.

of "the soft, small voice of the within." But man's ego and ego-centric desires force him to desobey the ringing voice of the Lord and such a one pursues a life of base vulgarity, seeking sense-gratification and ultimately bringing himself down to be punished by his own uncontrolled emotions and unchastened ideas. Hence the warning: "*You shall perish.*"

To weave the idea into the very warp and woof of Arjuna's *life, the Lord says:*

यदहंकारमाश्रित्य न योत्स्य इति मन्यसे ।
मिथ्यैष व्यवसायस्ते प्रकृतिस्त्वां नियोक्ष्यति ।।५९।।

Yad-ahaṁkāram-āśritya na yotsya iti manyase,
mithyaiṣa vyavasāyas-te prakṛtis-tvām niyokṣyati.

यत् *yat* = if; अहंकारम् *ahaṁkāram* = egoism; आश्रित्य *āśritya* = having taken refuge in; न योत्स्य *na yotsya* = (I) will not fight; इति *iti* = thus; मन्यसे *manyase* = (you) think; मिथ्या *mithyā* = vain; एषः *eṣaḥ* = this; व्यवसायः *vyavasāyaḥ* = resolve; ते *te* = your; प्रकृतिः *prakṛtiḥ* = nature; त्वाम् *tvām* = your; नियोक्ष्यति *niyokṣyati* = will compel.

59. Filled with egoism, if you think, "I will not fight," vain is this, your resolve; (for) nature will compel you.

General statements of truth are too volatile to be retained in one's understanding permanently. But the general statements of life's principles, when woven into the texture of one's own experiences, remain as one's own earned "knowledge," and they become permanent *wisdom.* Therefore, *Kṛṣṇa* is trying to bring the philosophical contents of his discourse into the very substance of *Arjuna's* own immediate problem.

Due to a sense of self-importance, if the self-conceited *Arjuna* were to think "*I will not fight,*" he shall be thinking so in vain! The temperament of *Arjuna* must seek its expression, and being a *Kṣatriya* of "passionate" nature, his *Rajoguṇa* will assert itself; "*nature will compel you.*" One who has eaten salt must feel terribly thirsty, ere long. The false arguments raised by *Arjuna* for not fighting the battle are all compromises made by his ego with the situation.

Even if he were to follow his temporary attitude of escapism and desist from fighting, it is a law of nature that his mental temperament would asset itself at a later period, when, alas! he may not have the field to express himself in and exhaust his *vāsanā-s.*

Also, because of the following reason 'You must fight.'

स्वभावजेन कौन्तेय निबद्धः स्वेन कर्मणा ।
कर्तुं नेच्छसि यन्मोहात् करिष्यस्यवशोऽपि तत् ।।६०।।

Svabhāvajena kaunteya nibaddhaḥ svena karmaṇā,
kartuṁ necchasi yan-mohāt kariṣyasya-vaśo'pi tat.

स्वभावजेन *svabhāvajena* = born of (your) own nature; कौन्तेय *kaunteya* = *O Kaunteya;* निबद्धः *nibaddhaḥ* = bound; स्वेन *svena* = (your) own; कर्मणा *karmaṇā* = by action; कर्तुम् *kartum* = to do; न *na* = not; इच्छसि *icchasi* = (you) wish; यत् *yat* = that; मोहात् *mohāt* = through delusion; करिष्यसि *kariṣyasi* = (you) shall do; अवशः *avaśaḥ* = helpless; अपि *api* = also; तत् *tat* = that.

60. O Son of Kuntī, *bound by your own Karma (action), born of your own nature, that which, through delusion you wish not to do, even that you shall do, helplessly.*

Continuing, the Lord, in effect, says: "I am asking you to fight, not because I have no pesonal sympathies for you, but because that is the only course left for you. You have no other choice. Though you now insist that you "*will not fight,*" it is merely an illusion. You will have to fight, because, your nature will assert itself."

The actions, we do, are propelled by our own *vāsanā-s* and they shackle our personality. *Arjuna* is essentially of the *Rajoguṇa* type, and therefore, he must fight. The *Pāṇḍava* Prince cannot, all of a sudden, pose to have the beauties of the *Sāttvik* nature of heart and retire to a solitary place to live a serene life of steady contemplation and come to experience the consequent self-unfoldment.

Because of wrong thinking and mis-calculations, Arjuna feels that he does not like war, and therefore, he is not ready to face it. But in spite of his determination, he will be compelled to fight by his own nature, ordered by the existing *vāsanā-s* in him. This is the irrevocable law of life.

He who has no control over his mind becomes a victim of circumstances. He gets thrown up and down by the whim and fancy of things around him. But he who gains inner mastery over the mind and stands firmly rooted and unshaken by the circumstances is the one who will revel (*Rati*) in the Pure Light (*Bhā*) of wisdom;* and the country that recognises this nature has acquired its immortal name '*Bharāta.*'

---

* Add hence the name of India is '*Bhā-rata.*'

The eighteenth Chapter of the *Gītā* can be considered as enunciating a philisophy to which the earlier seventeen cahpters are but so many brilliant arguments. The greater the control of the mind administered by the intellect, the nobler is that man; and the texture and nature of the great man will depend upon the nature of values that his intellect has learnt to acquire and respect in life.

In the previous two or three stanzas, we are told by *Kṛṣṇa*, "*Remember Me constantly.*" What does this mean? How should we remember? Does it mean meditating upon the Lord? What should be our relationship with Him? Are we to remember Him as a historical event, or remember Him as intimately connected with us as a 'Presence' expressing Itself at all times in and through us?

All these questions are apt to rise up in any serious student. And they are answered in the following:

ईश्वरः सर्वभूतानां हृद्देशेऽर्जुन तिष्ठति ।
भ्रामयन्सर्वभूतानि यन्त्रारूढानि मायया ।।६१।।

īśvaraḥ sarva-bhūtānāṁ hṛd-deśe-'rjuna tiṣṭhati.
bhrāmayan-sarva-bhūtāni yantrā-ruḍhāni māyayā.

ईश्वरः *Īśvaraḥ* = the Lord; सर्व-भूतानाम् *sarva-bhūtānām* = of all beings; हृद्देशे *hṛddeśe* = in the hearts; अर्जुन *Arjuna* = *O Arjuna;* तिष्ठति *tiṣṭhati* = dwells; भ्रामयन् *bhrāmayan* = causing to revolve; सर्व-भूतानि *sarva-bhūtāni* = all beings; यन्त्र आरूढानि *yantra-āruḍhāni* = mounted on a machine; मायया *māyayā* = by illusion.

61. The Lord dwells in the hearts of all beings, O Arjuna, causing all beings, by His illusive power, to revolve, as if mounted on a machine.

The advice given by the Lord is clear and beyond all shades of doubt. "Remember the Lord," says *Gītācārya*, "as the One who organises, controls and directs all things in the world and without Whose command nothing ever happens. In His 'presence' alone everything can happen-therefore remember Him as *Īśvara*." The steam functioning in the cylinder of the engine is the "Lord" of the engine, and without it, the piston can never move. It is the steam which provides the locomotion and renders the train dynamic.

Do not remember the Lord as merely a personified Power, as *Śiva* in *Kailāśa*, as *Viṣṇu* in *Vaikunṭha*, as the Father in Heaven etc., but recognise Him as one who dwells in the heart of everyone. Just as the address of a person is given, in order that the seeker of that person may locate the individual in a busy town, so also in order to seek, discover and identify with the Lord, His "Local address" is being provided here by *Bhagavān Kṛṣṇa*!

When we say that *"the Lord dwells in the heart of all living beings,"* we do not mean the physical heart. In philosophy the use of the word "heart" is more figurative than literal. It is something like our saying that this individual has a "*Large Heart" or a "good heart*", all that we mean is that the individual in question is a "man of love and human qualities."

Residing thus in the heart: meaning, in the mind of one who has cultivated the divine qualities such as love, kindness, patience, cheer, affection, tenderness, forgiveness, charity etc. The Lord lends His Power to all living creatures to act on. He energizes everyone. Everything revolves around Him-like the unseen hand that manipulates the dolls in the marionetteplay. The puppets have no existence, no vitality, no emotions of their own; they are only the expressions of the will and intention of the unseen hand behind them.

It is not the *matter* in us that moves or becomes conscious of the world of transactions; or else the cucumber and the pumpkin, the corn and the tomato of which our bodies are made, will also have locomotion or Consciousness. When the same vegetables are consumed as food and are digested and assimilaed to become part of our physical body, the *matter*, in contact with the Life-Principle in us becomes vibrant and dynamic, capable of perceiiving, feeling and thinking. The Spark-of-Life presiding over the body, the Pure Eternal Consciousness, is that which, as it were , vitalises inert *matter*. Pure Consciousness in itself does not act; but in Its Presence the *matter*-envelopments get vitalised, and act.

The *Atman*, conditioned by the body, mind and intellect, express dynamism and action, and creates what we recognise as the manifested individuality. "The Supreme functioning through the total bodies as the cause of all action" is called *Īśvara*.* Life functioning in each one of us is the master, the controller, the director and the Lord of our individual activities.

The essential Life in all of us is one and the same; therefore; the Total Life functions through and manifests as the entire Universe, energising all existing equipments. Thus expressing through all activities, is the Lord of the Universe, *Īśvara*.. With this understanding, if you read the stanza again, you will comprehend the metaphor employed

---

* *Samaṣti-kāraṇa-śarīra-abhimāṇi-īśvaraḥ.*

herein.

If there be, thus, a Lord within, meaning a power that rules over and guides all my activities, what are my responsibilities and duties towards Him?

तमेव शरणं गच्छ सर्वभावेन भारत ।
तत्प्रसादात्परां शान्तिं स्थानं प्राप्स्यसि शाश्वतम् ॥६२॥

Tameva śaraṇaṁ gaccha sarva-bhāvena bhārata,
tat-prasādāt-parāṁ śāntiṁ sthānaṁ prāpsyasi śāśvatam.

तम् *tam* = to him; एव *eva* = even; शरणम् गच्छ *śaraṇam gaccha* = take refuge; सर्वभावेन *sarva-bhāvena* = with all thy being; भारत *bhārata* = *O Bhārata*; तत्-प्रसादात् *tat-prasādāt* = by His grace; पराम् *parām* = supreme; शान्तिम् *śāntim* = peace; स्थानम् *sthānam* = the abode; प्राप्स्यसि *prāpsyasi* = (you) shall obtain; शाश्वतम् *śāśvatam* = eternal.

62. *Fly unto Him for refuge with all your being, O Bhārata; by His grace you shall obtain Supreme Peace (and) the Eternal Abode.*

Such an elaborate description has been given of the Spiritual Presence which vitalises the world-of-*matter* around man, only to bring about ultimately an evolutionary self-development in the student. The very core of this *Gītā*-philosophy is the theme that is indicated in the opening stanza of the *Īśāvāsya Upaniṣad.* "The Infinite Truth pervades everything in the world, and threfore, renouncing all the multiplicity, enjoy the Infinitude, and covet not anybody's wealth."*

* See *Svāmījī's* Discourses on *Īśāvāsyopaniṣad.* While reading the commentary upon this *mantra* in the *Upaniṣad,* please see that you glance through the commentaries upon the 'Peace Invocation' of the same *Upaniṣad* which comes prior to the *mantra.*

Recognition of the body through our abject identifications with it, creates a false sense of individuality, and it is this "ego" that suffers and sighs. The one commandment that has been repeated all through the Divine Song with great insistence is: "*Renounce the ego and act.*" The ego is the cause for all our sense of imperfections and sorrows. To the extent we liquidate this sense of separateness and individuality, to that extent we climb into an experience of greater perfection and joy within ourselves.

Kṛṣṇa has been advising surrender of the "ego" unto the Lord by developing a devoted attitude of dedication. Arjuna, like a true intelligent sceptic, asks: "To which Lord should I renounce all my action?-and dedicate all my activities at which altar? *Kṛṣṇa* has defined the Infinite Lord in the previous verse, and now, here He advises Arjuna to surrender his "ego" unto him. "*Fly unto Him for refuge with all your will.*"

Ours is an age of scepticism. The *Arjuna* of the *Gītā* is rather like a typical representative of our own age in this respect. A sceptic is one who questions the existing beliefs; he wants to be intellectually convinced of the logical grounds upon which the existing beliefs stand.*

Earlier, *Kṛṣṇa* has explained to Arjuna what is indicated by the term *Īśvara.* Now the call of the *Gītā* to *Arjuna* is to surrender himself unto the Lord. The *Gītā* requires

---

* As a contrast to the sceptic, the atheist is one so dull and under-developed in his evolution that the poor man is trying to live a mere animal life even though he is in the physical form of a man. His goal in life is mere satisfaction in momentary joys, gained while he gratifies and soothens his nerve tips. He has not yet got an awakened heart or head to feel the majesty and glory of life, or to think and question the existence of faith and its basis.

all of us to live and act with our hearts resting in self-dedicated surrender to the Consciousness, the harmonious oneness of Life that pulsates everywhere through all equipments. In short, we are asked to identify ourselves with the Spirit rather than the vehicles of Its expression He who has thus surrendered totally *(Sarva-bhāvena)* gains an intellect fully awakened, and thereafter, external circumstances cannot toss and crush his individuality.

The body and mind of such an individual who has learnt ever to keep the refreshing memory of the present cannot make any foolish demands. And when one brings such a brilliant intellect into the affairs of life, all his problems wither away and carpet his path to strive progressively ahead.

To the extent we identify ourselves with Him, to that extent His light and power become ours, and they are called "His Grace" (*Prasāda*). Ere long, as a result of this "grace" accumulated within, through the integration of the personality and constant surrender of the ego, the individual shall obtain "*the supreme Peace, the eternal resting place.*"

With one's all being (*Sarva-bhāvena*): This surrender unto the Lord should not be a temporary self-deception. We must grow into a consciousness of the Presence of the Divine in all the planes of our existence. To illustrate such a total devotion, we have the examples of *Rādhā, Hanumān, Prahlāda,* and others. Without bringing all the levels of our being, and all the facets of our personality, into our love for Him, we cannot drown our finite ego-sense into the joyous lap of the Infinite Lord. Thus, a true devotee must re-orientate his being and must surrender himself as a willing vehicle for His expression. Then and then alone, all the delusions end, and the mortal gains divine experience, and comes to live fully the State of Immortality of the Godhood.

In conclusion *Kṛṣṇa* adds:

इति ते ज्ञानमाख्यातं गुह्याद्गुह्यतरं मया ।
विमृश्यैतदशेषेण यथेच्छसि तथा कुरु ।।६३।।

Iti te jñānam-ākhyātaṁ guhyād-guhya-taraṁ mayā,
vimṛśyai-tad-aśeṣeṇa yathecchasi tathā kuru.

इति *iti* = thus; ते *te* = to you; ज्ञानम् *jñānam* = wisdom; आख्यातम् *ākhyātam* = has been declared; गुह्यात् *guhyāt* = than all secret; गुह्यतरम् *guhyataram* = greater (more) secret; मया *mayā* = by Me; विमृश्य *vimṛśya* = having reflecting upon; एतत् *etat* = this; अशेषेण *aśeṣeṇa* = fully; यथा *yathā* = as; इच्छसि *icchasi* = (you) choose; तथा *tathā* = so; कुरु *kuru* = act;

63. *Thus, the "Wisdom" which is a greater secret than all secrets, has been declared to you by Me; having reflected upon it fully, you now act as you choose.*

This can be considered as the closing verse of the *Gītā* discourses on the battle-field of *Kurukṣetra.* The word "thus" (*Iti*) is generally used in *Samskṛta* to indicate what we mean now a days, by the phrase "quotation closes." The Lord has ended His discourses here. The *Gītācārya* has by now declared the 'essential features of the entire *Hindu* view and way of life. There is nothing more for the teacher to add.

Greater secret than all secrets (Guhyāt-Guhyataram) :- A secret can be so called only as long as it is not divulged. The moment we come to know of a thing it is no longer a secret at all. The spiritual truth and the right way-of-living as discussed in the *Gītā* are termed as "*the secrets of all secrets*" in the sense that it is not easy for one to know the *Gītā* way of dynamic life and the *Gītā* vision-of-Truth, unless one is intiated into them. Even a subtle intellect, very efficient in knowing the material world, both in its arrangement of things and their mutual inter-action, must necessarily fail to feel the presence of this Subtle, Eternal and Infinite Self.

***Guhyam* :-** This is a term that has gone into much misuse and abuse in India in our recent past. The term was misconstrued to mean that the spiritual knowledge, which is the core of our culture, is a great secret to be carefully preseved and jealously guarded by the privileged few against anybody else coming to learn it. This orthodox view has no sanction in the scriptures, if we read them with the same large-heartedness of The *Ṛṣi-s*, who gave them to us. No doubt, there are persons who have not the intellectual vision, nor the mental steadiness nor the physical discipline to understand correctly this great Truth in all its subtle implications, and therefore, this is kept away from them lest they should come to harm themselves by falsely living a mis-understood philosophy.

***Reflect over it all* :-** Any amount of listening cannot make one gain in "wisdom." The knowledge gained through reading or listening must be assimilated and brought within the warp and the woof of our understanding; then alone can knowledge become wisdom. therefore, *Arjuna* is asked not to tamely accept *Kṛṣṇa's* Song of Life as truth, but he has been asked to independently think over all that the Lord has declared. To put the ideas between the mind and the intellect and to chew them properly is "reflection." Each one will have to get his own individual confirmation from his own bosom.

Thereafter act as you please :- *Kṛṣṇa* ultimately leaves the decision to act, the will to live the higher life, to Arjuna's own choice. Each one must reach the Lord by his own free choice. There is no compulsion; for, spontaneity is an invaluable requisite for all new births. Caesarian operation is dangerous very often both for the child and for the mother; proselytisation is always dangerous both for the Church as well as for the new convert. There is no complusion in *Hinduism.* We can train the plant, trim it to beauty, serve it with fertilising waters, keep it in the required sunlight, but we cannot force a bud to yield its fragrance right now. Similarly, a human personality cannot be forced by complusion to grow in its moral and ethical beauty or in its spiritual unfoldment.

In fact, an artist can thrive only in freedom and never under shackles. The *Hindu* has been called upon to think independently and come to his own conclusions. Certain directions are pointed out in order to make them contemplate but each must come to his own understanding. If it is forced down as a discipline on the people, there is a chance that religion would become a physical discipline rather than an inner unfoldment. Hence *Kṛṣṇa* suggests to *Arjuna;* "Do as you choose to act"- after fully reconsidering the way of life and the goal indicated by him so far in his Song Divine.

Man is ever free to reject or accept the Call Divine, but there is no question of a generation being *driven* into religion; according to the *Hindū* way of thought, the aspirants of culture must be individually drawn towards the higher way of life. True spiritual masters will not, and should not, persuade their generation through violence, miracles, and false promises. A true prophet will not accept any false responsibility; he will only constantly counsel his generation, but never will he compel.

Fanatic bigotry has caused untold human miseries. A thoughtless generation, under the false persuasions of the priest class, is often pushed forward to commit murders in the name of holy wars. This is possible only when the general mass of devotees is kept in utter ignorance, and is made to blindly believe, without any independent thinking, what the prophets or the teachers have said.

On the other hand, here you will find in the very symbolism of the *Gītā*-scene that *Kṛṣṇa*, the teacher, is a mere charioteer ready to drive the chariot in any direction to which *Arjuna*, the master, shall command, *Kṛṣṇa* bears no weapon; he has no war to wage. He has nothing to gain or to lose in the fields of *Kurukṣetra*. Yet, it is His duty to bring to the notice of His 'master' certain points of view, certain varieties which *Arjuna* seems to have not cared to recognise, or has over-looked because of the peculiar mental condition in which he was then. Having placed before him all the facts and figures of life, principles and methods of living, *Kṛṣṇa* rightly invities *Arjuna* to make his own independent decision after considering all these points. Spiritual teachers should never compel. And in India there has never been any form of indoctrination.

Devotion to the Lord is the secret of success in Karma Yoga. This is explained in the following :

सर्वगुह्यतमं भूयः शृणु मे परमं वचः।
इष्टोऽसि मे दृढमिति ततो वक्ष्यामि ते हितम् ॥६४॥

Sarva-guhya-tamam bhūyaḥ śṛṇu me paramaṁ vacaḥ,
iṣṭo-'si me dṛḍham-iti tato vakṣyāmi te hitam.

सर्व गुह्य-तमम् *sarva guhya-tamam* = the most secret of all; भूयः *bhūyaḥ* = again; शृणु *śṛṇu* = hear; मे *me* = my; परमम् *Paramam* = supreme; वचः *vacaḥ* = word; इष्टः *iṣṭaḥ* = beloved; असि *asi* = (you) are; मे *me* = of Me; दृढम् *dṛḍham* = dearly (lit. firm): इति *iti* = thus; ततः *tataḥ* = therefore; वक्ष्यामि *vakṣyāmi* = (I) will speak; ते *te* = your; हितम् *hitam* = what is good.

64. Hear again My supreme word, most secret of all; because you are dearly beloved of Me; therefore, I will tell you what is good (for you).

When the Lord has concluded His entire discourse with the words, "*the wisdom has been declared to you by me; now do as you please.*" *Arjuna*, who has been all along devotedly and attentively listening to the expounded philosophy, seems to register an expression of confusion on his face. *Arjuna* wants to get some more instructions.* The *Pāṇḍava* Prince, perhaps, feels that he has not fully assimilated the deep and intimate philosophy of life as expounded by the Lord. Therefore, *Kṛṣṇa* continues, "*Again I will repeat the profoundest wisdom; please,*

---

* An identical situation we find in the closing pages of *Kenopaniṣad* where, when everything has been declared, the student requests the teacher : 'Teach me the knowledge of *Brahman,'* whereupon the teacher declares that he has said all that he has to say. And yet, he adds on a few more *mantra-s* prescribing the discipline that is unavoidable for a beginner--see *Svāmījī's* Discourses on *Kenopaniṣad* .

Arjuna, listen again to this supreme wisdom."

The motive force behind every teacher coming out into the world to preach, to explain and to expound, is his abundant love for mankind. *Kṛṣṇa* repeats here the salient factors of his philosophical goal and the means of realising it, to *Arjuna*, "*because you are dearly beloved of me,*" meaning "you are my firm friend." For this reason, *Kṛṣṇa* tries to recapitualte his scheme of right living and noble endeavour in brief.

Arjuna is by temperament a soldier; and a soldier's intellect has no patience with a dialectical discourse. What he can best appreciate is only a cut-and-dried order shouted at him, and he has been trained by his vocation always to follow it implicitly. Reports and memoranda confuse the soldier; he is conditioned by his active nature and military training to obey implicitly precise orders shot at him in crisp words. *Arjuna* is expecting *Kṛṣṇa* to recast the whole philosophy into a precise, definite, decisive commandment. Understanding this silent demand of the soldier's heart, *Kṛṣṇa* promises here that He shall now declare the truth which is "the most secret of all" (*Sarva-guhya-tamam*).

What is it?

मन्मना भव मद्भक्तो मद्याजी मां नमस्कुरु ।
मामेवैष्यसि सत्यं ते प्रतिजाने प्रियोऽसि मे।। ६५।।

Manmanā bhava mad-bhakto madyājī māṁ namaskuru,
mām-evaiṣyasi satyaṁ te pratijāne priyo-si me.

मन्मना: *manmanāḥ* = with mind fixed on Me; भव *bhava* = be; मद्भक्त: *mad-bhaktaḥ* = devoted to Me; मद्याजी

madyājī = sacrifice to (worship) Me; माम् *mām* = to Me; नमस्कुरु *namaskuru* = bow down; माम् *mām* = to Me; एव *eva* = even; एष्यसि *eṣyasi* = (you) shall come; सत्यम् *satyam* = truth; ते *te* = to you; प्रतिजाने *pratijāne* = (I) promise; प्रियः *priyaḥ* = dear; असि *asi* = (you) are; मे *me* = of Me.

65. Fix your mind upon Me; be devoted to Me; sacrifice to Me; bow down to Me; you shall come, surely then, to Me alone; truly do I promise to you, (for) you are dear to Me.

A successful philosopher working in the field of renaissance in any age of utter decadence cannot avoid repeating again and again the fundamental points that constitute the framework of his philosophy because explanations have got a knack of veiling the main principles behind the mist of words. And yet, without elucidating explanations, the fundamental ideas cannot be hammered in. No nail can be driven home by soft persuasion; but it is to be remorselessly banged in by a hammer. Ideas can not penerate a confused head unless they are forced in by the sledge-hammer blows of repetition. This is the systematic method adopted in all *Śāstra-s. Kṛṣṇa* therefore, repeats here the salient features of the philosophy of the *Gītā* for the benefit of his student.

Four conditions are laid down for a successful seeker; and to those who have accomplished them all in themselves, an assurance of realisation, "*you shall reach me*," is given here. When a philosophy is summarised and enumerated in a few points, it has a deceptive look of utter simplicity, and a student is apt to take it lightly, or ignore it in toto. In order to avoid such a mistake, the teacher invariably endorses his statement that it is indeed all Truth: *I promise you truly."*

To add a punch to this personal endorsement, *Kṛṣṇa* guarantees the motive behind His discourses: " *You are dear to me."* Love is the correct motive force behind all spiritual teachings. Unless a teacher has infinite love for the taught, there is no inspired joy in teaching; a professional teacher is, at best, only a wage earner. He can neither inspire the student nor, while teaching, come to experience within himself the joyous ecstasy of satisfaction and fulfilment, which are the true rewards of teaching.

A substantial part of the philosophy and the "path" declared herein have already been taught in an earleir chapter (IX-34). And the same thing is repeated here with the endorsement that what He is declaring is no pleasant compromise but the total un-adulterated truth.

With the mind fixed on Me **:-** Meaning "ever remembering Me, ever devotedly identifying with Me" through the process of dedicating all your activities unto Me, in an attitude of reverence unto the All-pervading Life, if you work in the service of the world, the promise is that you will reach the Supreme Goal.

In all other religions the Goal is other than the Prophet; only in the *Gītā* the Supreme Himself is advising the seeker, and therefore He has to declare: " *You will reach Me."*

Looking up to *Vāsudeva* alone as your aim, means and end, "you shall reach Me." Knowing that the Lord's declarations are true, and being convinced that liberation is a necessary result of devotion to the Lord, one should look up to the Lord as the highest and the sole refuge.

The maladjusted "ego" in us has, by its own false concepts and imaginations, spooled us all up into cocoons of confusion and has tied us down with our own self-created shackles. Now, it is up to us to snap these cords that bind us and gain freedom from them all. The All-perfect Supreme has been, as though, shackled by our mind and intellect, and now the same mind and intellect must be utilised to unwind the binding cords. If we lock ourselves up in a room, it is left to us only to unlock its doors and walk out into freedom. *Vāsanā-s* are created by our ego-centric activities (*Sakāma-Karma*) and by self-less work (*Niṣkāma-Karma*) alone can these *Vāsanā-s* be ended. Therefore, *Kṛṣṇa* advises us: "Act on with mind fixed on Me. Devotedly work for Me. Dedicate all your activities as a sacrifice, as an offering unto Me."

An attitude of reverence to the Supreme is necessary in order to re-incorporate into the texture of our own life, the qualities of the Supreme. Like water, knowledge also flows only from a higher to a lower level. Therefore, our minds must be in an attitude of surrender to Him in utter reverence and devotion. When you work in the world with such an attitude, *Kṛṣṇa* says, "*you shall reach the Supreme.*"

A*ccording to* Śaṅkara, *"having taught, in conclusion, that the supreme secret of Karma Yoga is in regarding the Lord as the sole refuge,* Kṛṣṇa *now proceeds to speak of the infinite knowledge the fruit of Karma Yoga, as taught in the essential portion of all the* Upaniṣad-s":

सर्वधर्मान्परित्यज्य मामेकं शरणं व्रज ।
अहं त्वा सर्वपापेभ्यो मोक्षयिष्यामि मा शुचः ॥ ६६॥

Sarva-dharmān-parityajya mām-ekam śaraṇaṁ vraja,
aham tvā sarva-pāpebhyo mokṣa-yiṣyāmi mā śucaḥ

सर्व-धर्मान् *sarva-dharmān* = all *Dharma-s,* परित्यज्य *parityajya* = having abandoned; माम् *mām* = to Me; एकम् *ekam* = alone; शरणम् *śaraṇam* = refuge; व्रज *vraja* = take; अहम् *aham* = I; त्वा *tvā* = thee; सर्व-पापेभ्यः *sarva-pāpebhyaḥ* = from all sins; मोक्षयिष्यामि *mokṣa-yiṣyāmi* = will liberate; मा *mā* = not; शुचः *śucaḥ* = grieve.

66. *Abandoning all* Dharma-s *(of the body, mind, and intellect), take refuge in Me alone; I will liberate thee from all sins; grieve not.*

This is the noblest of all the stanzas in the Divine Song and this is yet the most controversial. Translators, reviewers, critics and commentators have invested all their originality in commenting upon this stanza, and various philosophers, each maintaining his own point of view, has ploughed the words to plant his ideas into the ample bosom of this great verse of brilliant import. To *Śrī Rāmānuja*, this is the final verse (*Carama-Śloka*) of the whole *Gītā.*

At least a few, if not many, of the translators have spoiled the beauty of the original, especially when their attempts were to render this verse into English. This is mainly because there is no equivalent term in any language of the world which can safely bear the total burden of the full import of the term *dharma*, as it is used in the *Hindu Śāstra-s.* The term mystifies any student of our religious text-books.

Most often used and yet in no two places having the same shade of suggestion, the term, '*Dharma*' has become the very heart of the *Hindu* culture. This explains why the religion of India was called by the people who lived in the land and enjoyed its spiritual wealth as the 'Sanatana Dharma.'

On our interpretation of the term dharma will depend upon our understanding of the Stanza. dharma, as used in our scriptures is, to put it directly and precisely, "the law of being." That because of which a thing continues to be the thing itself, without which the *thing* cannot continue to be that *thing*, is the *Dharma* of the thing. Heat, because of which fire maintains itself as fire, without which fire can no more be fire, is the *Dharma* of fire. Heat is the *Dharma* of fire; cold fire we have yet to come across! sweetness is the *Dharma* of sugar; sour sugar is a myth! Fluidity is the *Dharma* of water; solid water is a dream.

Every object in the world has two types of properties: (a) the essential, and (b) the non-essential. A substance can remain itself, intact, when its "non-essential" qualities are absent, but it cannot remain ever for a split moment without its "essential" property. The colour of the flame, the length and width of the tongues of flame, are all the "non-essential" properties of fire, but the essential property of it is 'heat.' This essential property of a substance is called its *Dharma.*

What exactly then is the *Dharma* of man? The colour of the skin, the innumerable endless varieties of emotions and thoughts-the nature, the conditions and the capacities of the body, mind and intellect-are the "non-essential" factors in the human personality, as against the Touch of Life, the Diving Consciousness, expressed through them all. Without the *Ātman* man cannot exist; it is truth which is the basis of existence. Therefore, the "essential *Dharma*" of man is the Divine Spark of Existence, the Infinite Lord.

With this understanding of the term Dharma, we shall appreciate its difference from mere ethical and moral rules of conduct, all duties in life, all duties towards relations, friends, community, nation and the world, all our obligations to our environment, all our affections, reverence, charity, and sense of goodwill-all that have been considered as our *Dharma* in our books. In and through such actions, physical, mental and intellectual, a man will bring forth the expression of his true *Dharma*-his Divine Status as the All-pervading Self. To live truly as the *Ātman*, and to express Its Infinite Perfection through all our actions and in all our contacts with the outer world is to rediscover our *Dharma*.

The Self is realised only when we have withdrawn our false identifications with the body, mind and intellect, Due to this clinging attachment to these vehicles, we are today expressing in our existence the *dharma-s* of these *matter*-made vehicles. We live as though we are the body, or we exist dancing to the tunes that are struck by the emotions in us, or we get ourselves kicked and played about here and there by our own intellects' unpredictable suggestions. Though in a sense man's essential nature-primary property-*dharma* is to be the infinite, divine, all-blissful *Ātman*, he behaves as though he is a mere composite of the physical, psychological, and intellectual beings. All the sorrows and agitations, regrets and disappointments, passions and pains are dividends paid by the body, mind and intellect to the false and the deluded indentifier-the ego.

If we have thus understood the word *dharma* in all its implications, then this most glorious stanza in the *Gītā* shall sing its song directly to us. There are, no doubt, a few other stanzas in the *Gītā* wherein the Lord has almost directly commanded us to live a certain way-of-life, and has promised that if we obey His instructions, He will directly take the responsibility of guiding us towards his own being. But nowhere has the Lord so directly and openly expressed His divine willingness to undertake the service of His devotee as in this stanza.

He wants the meditator to accomplish three distinct adjustments in his inner personality. They are :

(1) Renounce all Dharma-s through meditation:

(2) Surrender to My refuge alone; and while in the state of meditation;

(3) Stop all worries.

And as a reward Lord Krsna promises : "*I shall release you from all sins.*" This is a promise given to all mankind. The *Gītā* is a universal scripture; it is the Bible of Man, the Koran of Humanity, the dynamic scripture of the Hindū-s.

Abandoning all dharma-s (Sarva-Dharmān Parityajya) **:-** As we have said above, *Dharma* is "the law of being", and we have already noted that nothing can continue its existence when once it is divorced from its *Dharma.* And yet, *Kṛṣṇa* says, "*come to my refuge, after renouncing all dharma-s.*" Does it then mean that our definition of *Dharma* is wrong? Or is there a contradiction in this stanza? Let us see.

As a mortal, finite ego, the seeker is living, due to his identification with them, the Dharma-s of his body, mind and intellect, and exists in life as a mere perceiver, feeler, and thinker. The perceiver-feeler-thinker personality in us is the "individuality" which expresses itself as the "ego." These are not our 'essential' Dharma-s. And since these are the 'non-essentials,' "renouncing all dharma-s" means "ending the ego."

This is a stanza applicable while in the seat of meditation. The rest of the time also we can charter our way of life basing our attitude towards various things and beings upon the sacred suggestions in this loving commandment of the Lord. All disturbances in meditation arise out of the self asserting ego in us. In spite of ourselves, the meditator in us finds himself bumped out of his gathered tranquillity within onto the rough seas of our physical appetites or emotional cravings or intellectual demands.

"To renounce" therefore means "not to allow oursleves to fall again and again into this state of identification with the outer envelopments of matter around us." extrovert tendencies of the mind are to be renounced. "Develop introspection diligently" is the deep suggestion in the phrase "renouncing all dharma-s."

Come to Me alone for shelter (*Mām ekam Śaranam vraja*) :- Self-withdrawal from our extrovert nature will be impossible unless the mind is given a positive method of developing its introvert attention. By single-pointed, steady contemplation upon Me, the Self, which is the One-without-a-second, we can successfully accomplish our total withdrawal from the mis-interpreting equipments of the body, mind and intellect.[1]

1. We have, often, in the previous chapters explained the dynamic positivity of the *Hindu* approach to Truth.

The philosophers in India were never satisfied with a negative approach in their instructions; there are more do's than dont's with them. This practical nature of our philosophy, which is native to our traditions, is amply illustrated in this stanza when Lord *Kṛṣṇa* commands His devotees to come to His shelter whereby they can accomplish the renunciation of all their false identifications.

Be not grieved (*Mā śucaḥ*) :- When both the above conditions are accomplished, the seeker reaches a state of growing tranquillity in meditation. But it will all be a waste if this subjective peace, created after so much labour, were not to form a steady and firm platform for his personality to spring forth from, into the realms of the Divine Consciousness. The spring-board must stay under our feet, supply the required propulsion for our inward dive. But unfortunately, the very anxiety to reach the Infinite weakens the platform. Like a dream-bridge, it disappears at the withering touch of the anxieties in the meditator, During meditation, when the mind has been persuaded away from all its restless pre-occupations with the outer vehicles, and brought, again and again, to contemplate upon the Self, the Infinite, Lord *Kṛṣṇa* wants the seeker to renounce all his "*anxieties to realise.*"[2] Even a desire to realise is a disturbing thought that can obstruct the final achievement.

I shall release you from all sins :- That which brings about agitations in the bosom and thereby causes dissipation of the energies is called "sin." The actions themselves can

---

2. The same idea we have met with in chapter VI, stanza 25, when after explaining the ways of developing concentration, the Lord advised : *"Na kiñcid api Cintayet.'*

cause subtle exhaustions of the human power, as no action can be undertaken without bringing our mind and intellect into it. In short, the mind and intellect will always have to come and control every action. Actions thus leave their "foot prints," as it were, upon the mental stuff, and these marks which channelise the thought-flow and shape the psychological personality, when our mind has gone through its experiences, are called *vāsanā-s.*

Good *vāsanā-s* bring forth a steady stream of good thoughts as efficiently as bad *vāsanā-s* erupt bad thoughts. As long as thoughts are flowing, the mind survives-whether good or bad. To erase all *vāsanā-s* completely is to stop all thoughts i.e., the total cessation of thought-flow viz. "mind." Transcending the mind-intellect-equipment is to reach the plane of Pure Consciousness, the *Kṛṣṇa*-Reality.

As a seeker renounces more and more of his identifications with his outer envelopments through a process of steady contemplation and meditation upon the Lord of his heart, he grows in his vision. In the newly awakened sensitive consciousness, he becomes more and more poignantly aware of the numebr of *vāsanā-s* he has to exhaust. "Be not grieved," assures the Lord, for, "*I shall release you from all sins*"-the distrubing, thought-gurgling, action-prompting, desire-breeding, agitation-brewing *vāsanā-s* the "sins."

The stanza is important in as much as it is one of the most powerfully worded verses in the *Gītā* wherein the Lord, the Infinite, personally undertakes to do something helpful for the seeker in case the spiritual hero in him is ready to offer his ardent co-operation and put forth his best efforts. All through the days of seeking, a *Sādhaka* can asure himself steady progress in spirituality only when he is able to keep within himself a salubrious mental climate of warm optimism. To despair and to weep, to feel dejected and disappointed, is to invite restlessness of the mind, and naturally, therefore, spiritual unfoldment is never in the offing. The stanza, in its deep imports and wafting suggestions, is indeed a peroration in itself of the entire philosophical poem, the *Gītā.*

Having concluded the entire doctrine of the Gītā Śāstra *in this discourse, and having also briefly and conclusively restated the doctrine in order to impress it more firmly, the Lord proceeds now to state the rule that should be borne in mind while imparting this knowledge to others:*

इदं ते नातपस्काय नाभक्ताय कदाचन ।
न चाशुश्रूषवे वाच्यं न च मां योऽभ्यसूयति।। ६७।।

Idaṁ te nātapaskāya nā-bhaktāya kadācana,
na cāśuśrūṣave vācyaṁ na ca māṁ yo-'bhyasūyati.

इदम् *idam* = this; ते *te* = by you; न *na* = not; अतपस्काय *atapaskāya* = to one who is devoid of austerity; न *na* = not; अभक्ताय *abhaktāya* = to one who is not devoted; कदाचन *kadācana* = never; न *na* = not; च *ca* = and; अशुश्रूषवे *āśuśrūṣave* = to one who does not render service, or who desires not to listen; वाच्यम् *vācyam* = to be spoken; न *na* = not; च *ca* = and; माम् *mām* = me; यः *yaḥ* = who; अभ्यसूयति *abhyasūyati.* = cavils at (talks ill of Me).

67. *This is never to be spoken by you to one who is devoid of austerities or devotion, nor to one who does*

not render service, nor to one who desires not to listen, nor to one who cavils at Me.

In almost all scriptural texts we find, in their closing stanzas, a description of the type of students to whom this knowledge can be imparted. Following faithfully this great tradition, here also we have this enumeration of the necessary qualifications for a true student of the *Gītā.* These are not so many fortresses raised round the treasure-house of the *Gītā* in order to protect some interests and provide some people with a kind of monopoly in trading upon the wealth of ideas in these discourses. On the other hand, we shall find that these qualifications are essential adjustments in the inner personality of the student. And a bosom so tuned up is the right vehicle that can daringly invest that knowledge in living one's life and thus earn the 'joy-of-wisdom.'

Since these are the adjustments that are necessary within a student, it also implies that he who fails to appreciate fully the contents of the *Gītā* can come to polish his instruments better if he tries to cultivate these very same qualities. In short, the stanza under discussion tells us of those who cannot be benefited by the study of the *Gītā.*

Those who do not live an austere life:- Those who do not have any control over their body and mind, who have dissipated their physical and mental energies in the wrong direction and have thus become impotent bodily, mentally and intellectually-to them "*never is this to be spoken by you,*" for, it will not be beneficial to them. There is not a trace of prejudice in this stanza. It is equivalent to saying "please do not sow seeds upon rocks" for the sower will never be able to reap, as nothing can grow on rocks.

Tapas is a practice of self-denial so that the energies that are dissipated through indulgence are conserved and intelligently redirected to win the ampler fields of spiritual unfoldment. *Tapas* is, therefore, a plan which consists of:

(1) conservation of all energies wasted, meaning economisation of the expenditure of energy;

(2) preservation of the energies so saved; and

(3) redirection and re-employing of this new found energies in the constructive fields of self-unfoldment.

Those who are not practising tapas are not really fit to court and gain the loving embrace of the rejuvenating philosophy in the *Gītā.*

Those who have no devotion :- That is, those who do not have the capacity to identify themselves with the ideal that they want to reach. If one cannot sympathise with an ideal, one can much less absorb or assimilate it. An ideal, however well understood intellectually, cannot yield its full benefit unless it is expressed in life. To hug on to the ideal, in a clasp of love, is devotion.

Those who do not render service :- We have seen earlier, almost in all chapters, *Kṛṣṇa* again and again instisting that selfless activity is not only a means for the *Sādhaka*, but it is at once also the field where the perfect Masters discover their fulfilment. Seekers who are not able to serve others, who are selfish, who have no human qualities, who have never felt a sympathetic love for others-such persons are merely consumers and not producers of joy for others, and they invaribaly fail to understand or appreciate or come to live the joys of the *Kṛṣṇa*-way-of-life.

Those who are cavilling at Me i.e., those who murmur against Me **:-** If we do not respect and revere our teacher we can never learn from him. The first person singular used in the *Gītā* is identical with the Self, the Goal, and therefore, it means, "*those who are not able to respect philosophy.*" Forceful conversion may enhance the numerical strength of a faith, but self-development and inner unfoldment cannot come that way. Religion should not be forced upon anyone. One who has mentally rejected a philosophy can never, even when one has understood it, live up to it. Therefore, those who are entertaining a secret disrespect for a philosophy should not be forced to study it.

Stanzas like this in a *Śāstra* are meant as instructions for the students on how to attune themselves properly so that they can make a profitable study of the *Śāstra.* None should expect an immediate result from his study of the *Gītā.* Personality readjustments cannot be made overnight. There is no miracle promised in the *Gītā.*

Indirectly, the stanza also gives some sane instructions by its suggestions. If a student feels that he cannot satisfactorily understand the *Gītā,* he has only to sharpen his inner nature further by the above subjective processes. Just as we cleanse a mirror to remove the dimness of the reflection, so too, by properly readjusting the mind-intellect-equipment, its sensitivity to absorb the *Gītā*-philosophy can be increased.

Now the Lord proceeds to state what benefits will accrue to him who hands down his knowledge to others in the society:

य इमं परमं गुह्यं मद्भक्तेष्वभिधास्यति ।
भक्तिं मयि परां कृत्वा मामेवैष्यत्यसंशयः ॥ ६८॥

Ya imaṁ paramaṁ guhyaṁ mad-bhakteṣv-abhidhāsyati,
bhaktiṁ mayi parāṁ kṛtvā mām-evaiṣyaty-asaṁśayaḥ.

यः *yaḥ* = who; इमम् *imam* = this; परमम् *paramam* = supreme; गुह्यम् *guhyam* = secret; मद्-भक्तेषु *mad-bhakteṣu* = my devotees; अभिधास्यति *abhidhāsyati* = shall declare, teach; भक्तिम् *bhaktim* = devotion; मयि *mayi* = in Me; पराम् *parām* = supreme; कृत्वा *kṛtvā* = having done; माम् *mām* = me; एव *eva* = even; एष्यति *eṣyati* = shall come; असंशयः *asamśayaḥ* = doubtless.

68. He who, with supreme devotion to Me, will teach this supreme secret to My devotees, shall doubtless come to Me.

The stanza under review and the following one are both glorifications of a teacher who can give the correct interpretation of the *Gītā* and make the listeners follow the *Kṛṣṇa*-way-of-life. "Fight the evil down, whether it be within or without" is the cardinal principle that *Kṛṣṇa* advocates to Prince *Arjuna.* In order to impart such a culture, it is not enough that the teacher be a mere scholar, but he must have the *Kṛṣṇa*-ability. Hence the glorification.

It is useless to impart this knowledge to those who have not taste for it. Hunger alone can lend taste to the food. If a student himself has not any sense of urgency for a total revolution in himself, he cannot be goaded to live the *Gītā-life.* The Lord's Song has a special appeal to those who have the mysterious spiritual thirst to live a fuller and more dynamic life. Hence it is said: "This deeply profound philosophy" (*Paramam Guhyam*) must be imparted to "My devotees" (*Madbhakteṣu*). Devotion to the Lord (*Bhakti*) means the capacity to identify with the ideal, and therefore, the philosophy of the ideal-way-of-life can profitably be imparted only to those persons who have a capacity to identify themselves with the ideal and thereafter live up to it.

It is not sufficient that the student alone has this capacity to identify himself with the higher ideal, but the teacher also must have (*Bhakti*) "perfect attunement" with the Supreme *Kṛṣṇa*-Reality. Such an individual, who is himself rooted in his atturement, and who tries to impart this knowledge to others and thereby constantly occupies himself in reflections upon the philosophical ideals of the *Gītā*-"shall certainly (*Asaṁśayaḥ*) come to Me alone."

This is in the correct spirit of the Upanisadik tradition. In the *Upaniṣad-s* also, we find the teachers insisting upon the glory in the spreading of the spiritual knowledge. In the *Taittirīya Upaniṣad* the very parting advice of the teacher to the taught contains an oft-reiterated injunction that he must practice, not only study of the scripture himself, but must continuously spend himself in carrying the torch of knowledge among the masses.* This has been prescribed as an imperative duty for all *brāhmaṇa-s* by the *Ṛṣi-s.*

An educated man should, in his gratitude, feel much indebted to the Muse-of-Wisdom. In fact, this indebtedness

---

* *Svādhyāya pravacanābhyām na pramaditavyam--Taittirīya Upaniṣad (I-xi-1).*

is actually called, in our tradition, *Ṛṣi*-indebtedness (*Ṛṣi-Ṛṇam*), to absolve ourselves from which, we are asked everyday to study their works and preach their ideas. When we lost these two great ideals, when the later *brāhmaṇa* generations conveniently forgot their duties and responsibilities, and thus disobeyed this glorious injunction of the great *Ṛṣi-s*, started our cultural decadence.

Philosophy is the basis of every culture. The *Hindu* culture can revive and assert its glory only when it is nurtured and nourished by the philosophy of India which is contained in the *Upaniṣad-s*. The fathers of our culture, the great *Ṛṣi-s*, knowing this secret, urged the students of the Scriptures not to keep this knowledge to themselves, but to import it freely to others. In this way alone the culture can be successfully brought into the dim-lit chambers of people's lives.

When a stone is thrown into a pond of water, it makes a disturbance which ripples out in concetric circles and widens itself to create many more ripples until the movement felt in the centre is progressively conveyed towards the outermost banks all around. If instead of water it is a basin of oil, the ripples made widen out and hide before they reach the banks. In case it is molten coal-tar, the stone makes a disturbance only at the point where it has struck the surface, and there it sinks to disappear leaving not a mark even on the surface. The disturbance gets no chance to ripple out its grace to any farther point.

From the above analogy, if a student, who has understood even a wee bit of our cultural tradition, does not convey it to others, it means that there is no mobility of intelligence or fluidity of inspiration in him. He who is thus capable of conveying the truths of the *Gītā* to others is complimented here with the promise of the highest reward: "*He shall doubt-less come to Me.*"

Not only this, but the Lord expresses that He loves such a teacher much more than anybody else:

न च तस्मान्मनुष्येषु कश्चिन्मे प्रियकृत्तमः ।
भविता न च मे तस्मादन्यः प्रियतरो भुवि ।। ६९ ।।

na ca tasmān-manuṣyeṣu kaścin-me priya-kṛttamaḥ,
bhavitā na ca me tasmād-anyaḥ priya-taro bhuvi.

न *na* = not; च *ca* = and; तस्मात् *tasmāt* = than he; मनुष्येषु *manuṣyeṣu* = among men; कश्चित् *kaścit* = any; मे *me* = of Me; प्रिय-कृत्तमः *priya-kṛttamaḥ* = one who does dearer (pleasing) service; भविता *bhavitā* = shall be; न *na* = not; च *ca* = and; मे *me;* = of Me; तस्मात् *tasmāt* = than he; अन्यः *anyaḥ* = another; प्रिय-तरः *priya-taraḥ* = dearer; भुवि *bhuvi* = on the earth.

69. Nor is there any among men who does dearer service to Me, nor shall there be another on earth dearer to Me than he.

In *Hindusim* there is no proselytism, it is true, we do not believe in compelling others to have faith in the Eternal Reality. Compulsion becomes a necessity where intellectual conversion is not possible. Since we have got a completely logical and entirely convincing philosophy which can generate in us our faith in the Ultimate, compuslion is no more needed. Human intellect has intrinsically such an honesty of conviction that once it has understood some way of life and has accepted certain values of life as a result of its understanding, it cannot but live its own convictions. It is only in this sense that the *Hindu* philosophy and our ancient teachers discarded proselytism and forceful conversion as barbarous methods not fitting the dignity of any truly spiritual system.

Unfortunately, this glorious creed has been so thoroughly misunderstood in India that we have long ago stopped our missionary work in propagating the immortal truths of our inimitable culture. Since the Christian missionaries act with the sole ambition of conversion, the educated Indian, in his thoughtless-ness has from his childhood on, associated these two ideas together in his mind. When he has understood the saner idea that proselytism is a crime against man and God, he seems to understand that missioanry work was never contemplated by the *Ṛṣi-s.* The stanza in the *Gītā* indeed gives the lie to such a fallacious conclusion.

To spread the idea among the people, to carry the torch of knowledge earlier lit up at the master's feet, to convey it far and wide to provide light wherever there is darkness, to keep oneself ever bubbling with an inspired enthusiasm, to pour out one's own convictions into the hearts of others-in short, vidyā-dāna is in *Hinduism,* a duty religiously imposed upon all students. Knowledge hoarded and secreted brings about a sadder poverty than the wealth aggrandised and cornered in a society.

All these ideas are beautifully brought out when *Kṛṣṇa* again takes up, in this stanza, the glorification of the teacher who teaches the *Gītā*-knowledge, Herein, *Kṛṣṇa* explains how such a man can reach Him easily, as declared in the previous verse. The *Gītācārya* emphasises that such an individual is "dearest to My heart, as I find none equal to him in the world." Not only is there none to compare with him amongst the present generation, but there shall never be (*Bhavitā-Na-Ca*) anyone, even in future times, so dear to Him, the Lord says, as such an individual who spends his time in spreading the knowledge of what little he has understood from the *Gītā.* A preacher* is sacred in the *Hindu* lore.

---

* In this context it is interesting to note how the elderly *Mahātmā-s* now living in the *Himālayan* valleys look at the missionary zeal of the young *Mahātmā-s.* Recently, I had to face one of the elderly *Mahātmā-s* in *Uttarakāśī.* When in conversation I reported to him, with a native enthusiasm and a sense of pardonable satisfaction, that my work of spreading the contents of our scriptures is being slowly recognised and appreciated by the younger generation, the ancient brows were slightly raised to express an impossible surprise. There was an excruciating silence for a few minutes; and my flow of words stopped the moment I saw the screaming criticism on those sacred brows. After a time the revered *Svāmījī* said : "*Chinmaya,* you better stay here now and no more need you go out in the world."

No doubt I was at a loss to understand what he meant. Explaining his idea, the revered *Svāmījī* continued after a pause : 'If you think that you are spreading these spiritual ideas, my boy, by the time you have spread the sacred ideals of *Vedānta* among the people, you will be a lost soul, because you will have by then developed a terrible amount of irrepressible ego! Our *Ācārya-s* have advised us that after *saṁnyāsa* we have only one sole duty in life-- to reflect upon truths of the scriptures and thus meditate upon the Infinite.'

How dissemination of knowledge would bloat one's ego, I was not convinced. When I expressed my inability to follow his line of thinking, that revered old saint of knowledge and wisdom kindly smiled, and patting me paternally on my back, said : 'Son, devotees might come and ask of us their doubts. You may give your discourses in the cities; there is none who is doing it now as you are. But one thing we should do: Never talk to the audience; talk to your own mind and make it a louder reflection in yourself to yourself. Thereby you will not only stop the growth of the ego in you but also will be talking to the mind and heart of your audience. May your missionary lectures and inspired preachings be a homely talk and a fruitful discussion between your own higher intellect and lower mind. If those who are around you are benefited by your own self-reflection, it shall be the glory of the Lord and not your personal 'efficiency.'

I was smothered down by the beauty and depth of significance of this sacred attitude of the ideal *Hindu* missionary in India. Glory to the *Ṛṣi-s.*

Earlier, in the *Gītā*, a great psychological truth has been hinted at, which is often repeated throughout the entire length of the Divine Song, and this cardinal secret is that he who can bring his entire mind to the contemplation of the Divine, to the total exclusion of all dissimilar thought-currents, will come to experience the Infinite Divine. A student of the *Gītā* who is spending his time in serious studies and in deep reflection upon them, and in preaching what he has understood, comes to revere the knowledge and thus reach an identification with an inner peace that is the essence of truth. Therefore, *Kṛṣṇa* says: "There can never be any other man more dear to Me by earnestly and devotedly trying to convey the immortal principles expounded in the *Gītā.*

It is not necessary in this context, that we must first ourselves become masters of the entire *Gītā*-knowledge. Whatever one has understood one must immediately, with an anxious love, give out to those who are completely ignorant. Also, one must sincerely and honestly try to live the principles in one's own life-"Such a man is dearest to Me."

Not only the preacher but even an ardent student is

congratulated in the following stanza:

अध्येष्यते च य इमं धर्म्यं संवादमावयोः ।
ज्ञानयज्ञेन तेनाहमिष्टः स्यामिति मे मतिः ॥ ७० ॥

Adhyeṣyate ca ya imaṁ dharmyaṁ saṁvādam-āvayoḥ,
jñāna-yajñena tenāham-iṣṭaḥ syāmiti me matiḥ.

अध्येष्यते *Adhyeṣyate* = Shall study; च *ca* = and; यः *yaḥ* = who; इमम् *imam* = this; धर्म्यम् *dharmyam* = sacred; संवादम् *samvādam* = dialogue; आवयोः *āvayoḥ* = of ours; ज्ञान-यज्ञेन *jñāna-yajñena* = by the sacrifice of wisdom; तेन *tena* = by him; अहम् *aham* = I; इष्टः *iṣṭaḥ;* = worshipped; स्याम् *syām* = (I) shall have been; इति *iti* = thus; मे *me* = my; मतिः *matiḥ* = conviction.

70. And he who will study this sacred dialogue of ours, by him I shall have been worshipped by the "sacrifice-of-wisdom," such is My conviction.

Having thus glorified all teachers of the *Gītā* who carry the "Wisdom-of-the-sacred-discourse" to the masses, the *Gītā*, here, is glorifying even the students who are studying this Sacred text of the Lord's Song. The great philosophy of life given out here as a conversation between *Kṛṣṇa*-the Infinite, and *Arjuna*-the finite, has such a compelling charm about it, that even those who read it superficially will also be slowly dragged into the very sanctifying depths of it. Such an individual is, even unconsciously, egged on to make a pilgrimage to the greater possibilities within himself, and naturally, he comes to evolve through what *Kṛṣṇa* terms here as "*Jñāna Yajña.*"

In our *Śastra-s*, sacrifices fall under four distinct categories:

(1) rituals (*vidhi*),

(2) Repetition (*japa*)

(3) Muttering or whispering (*upāṁśu*),

(4) Mental *(manasa).*

The wisdom-sacrifice' (*Jñāna yajña*) falls under the last category and, therefore, it is glorified.

In *Yajña,* Lord Fire is invoked in the sacrificial through and into it are offered oblations by the devotees. From this analogy, the term *Jñāna Yajña* has been originally coined and used in the *Gītā.* Study of the Scriptures and regular contemplation upon their deep significances kindle the "Fire-of-Knowledge" in us and into this the intelligent seeker offers, as his oblation, his own false values and negative tendencies. This is the significance of the metaphorical phrase *Jñāna Yajña.* Therefore, here the Lord admits but a truth in the Spiritual science when He declares that those who study the *Gītā*- contemplate upon its meaning, understand it thoroughly- and those who can, at the altars of their well-kindled understanding, sacrifice their own ego-centric misconceptions about themselves, and about the world around them, are certainly the greatest devotees of the Infinite.

There is a subtle difference between *reading* and *studying:* newspapers are read; market tendencies are *studied* by the man of this age. In *reading,* it is mainly an attempt to satisfy a curiosity of what the theme is, but the process of *study* is not only a thirst to *understand* the theme but a *hunger* to gain into ourselves the perfections discussed therein through reflection and practice.

When a rusted key is heated in fire, the rust falls off and the key regains its original brightness. So too, our personality, when reacted with the knowledge of the *Gītā*, is chastened, since our wrong tendencies, unhealthy *vāsanā-s* and false sense-of-ego which have risen from false-knowledge (*Ajñāna*), all get burnt up in Right-Knowledge (*Jñāna*).

After thus explaining so far the glory of the teacher and the benefits of study, in the following stanza Kṛṣṇa *indicates that even 'listening to the* Gītā *discourses is beneficial:*

श्रद्धावाननसूयश्च शृणुयादपि यो नरः ।
सोऽपि मुक्तः शुभाँल्लोकान्प्राप्नुयात्पुण्यकर्मणाम् ।। ७१ ।।

Śraddhāvān-anasūyaś-ca śṛṇuyād-api yo naraḥ,
so'pi muktaḥ śubhāṅ-llokān- prāpnuyāt-puṇya-karmaṇām.

श्रद्धावान् *śraddhāvān* = full of faith; अनसूयः *anasūyaḥ* = free from malice; च *ca* = and; शृणुयात् *śṛṇuyāt* = may hear; अपि *api* = also; यः *yaḥ* = who; नरः *naraḥ* = man; सः *saḥ* = he; अपिः *api* = also; मुक्तः *muktaḥ* = liberated; शुभान् *śubhān* = happy; लोकान् *lokān* = worlds; प्राप्नुयात् *prāpnuyāt* = shall attain; पुण्य-कर्मणाम् *puṇya-karmaṇām* = of those righteous deeds.

71. *The man also, who hears this, full of faith and free from malice, he too, liberated, shall attain to the happy worlds of those righteous deeds.*

The process of study of a text book dealing with the 'science of life' is different from the process of study adopted in all other scientific fields, Herein, in order to reach our fulfilment in the study, we must actually come to experience the excellences indicated by the teacher and the perfections promised by the *Ṛṣi-s.* that means we have to reach and understand, reflect and digest what we have gathered from our studies, assimilate this knowledge into an intimate conviction through attempts at living them and ultimately come to experience the very perfection which it promises.

In short, the student of the *Gītā* cannot stand apart from his text book, and merely learn to appreciate the theme of the Lord's Song. An all-out, ardent wooing of the *Gītā* by the student at all levels is necessary, if the study, of the *Gītā* is really to fulfil the student's spiritual unfoldment. Consequently, *Kṛṣṇa* indicates here two conditions, fulfilling which alone can one profitably listen to the *Gītā* discourses and hope to gather a large dividend of joy and perfection.

***Full of faith* (*Śraddhāvān*) :-** The term *Śraddhā* in *Samskṛta*, though usually translated as "faith," actually means much more than what it indicates in the English language and in the Western tradition. *Śraddhā* has been defined as "that faculty in the human intellect which gives it the capacity to dive deep into and discover the subtler meaning of the scriptural declarations, and thus helps the individual to absorb that understanding into the warp and the woof of his own intellect."*

Śraddhā is that faculty in the intellect which helps it:-

---

* See *Svāmījī's* talks on *Śaṅkara's Vivekacūḍāmaṇi: 'Śāstrasya guruvākyasya satya-bhuddhyā-vadhāraṇā sā śraddhā.'*
Faith--'Faith is the bird that feels the light and sings when the dawn is still dark.'--Tagore.

(1) to understand the subtle import of the sacred words:
(2) to absorb the same:
(3) to assimilate: and
(4) to make the student live up to those very same ideals.

Naturally, listening to the Lord's discourses can be fruitful only to those who have developed this essential faculty in themselves.

Free from malice (***Anasūyaḥ***) **:-** They alone who are free from malice against the teachings of the *Gītā* can undertake, with a healthy attitude of mind, a deeper and detailed study of it. No doubt, *Hinduism* never asks any student to read and study a philosophy with an implicit and ready faith. But the human mind, as it is, will grow dull and unresponsive when it has idle prejudices against the very theme of its study.

The intellect can receive the ideals preached in the *Gītā* only through the sense-organs, and these ideas must reach the intellect, filtered through the mind. If the mind contains any malice towards the very philosophy or the philosopher, the arguments and the goal indicated therein can never appeal to the student's intellect. No doubt, the student should bring in his own constructive criticism of an independent judgement upon what he studies, but he must be reasonably available to listen patiently to what the scripture has to say. In short, a student of religion must learn to keep an open mind and not condemn the philosophy before understanding what it has to say.

Such an individual who has attentively listened to the *Gītā*, who has intellectually absorbed, and assimilated the knowledge, "he too," says the Lord, "gets liberated" from the present state of confusions and sorrows, entanglements and bondages in his personality, and reaches a state of inner tranquillity and happiness.

***Joy is an inside job* :-** The kingdom of joy lies within all of us. Heaven is not somewhere yonder; it is here and now. Happiness and sorrow are both within us. To the extent we learn and live the principles of right living, as enunciated in the *Gītā,* to that extent, we shall come to gain a cultural eminence within ourselves and live an ampler life of greater achievements.

It is the duty of a teacher to see that the student understands the great Goal and the 'Path' completely. If the 'path' adivsed is found to be inadequate to bless the student, it is the duty of the teacher to find out ways and means of making the student discover his own balance.

Hence in the following stanza we find Kṛṣṇa *enquiring whether* Arjuna *has understood what He had expounded in thse eighteen chapters :*

कच्चिदेतच्छ्रुतं पार्थ त्वयैकाग्रेण चेतसा ।
कच्चिदज्ञानसंमोहः प्रनष्टस्ते धनंजय ।। ७२।।

kaccid-etac-chrutam pārtha tvayai-kāgreṇa cetasā,
kaccid-ajñāna-sammohaḥ pranaṣṭas-te dhanañjaya.

कच्चित् *kaccit* = whether; एतत् *etat* = this; श्रुतम् *śrutam* = heard; पार्थ *pārtha* = *O Pārtha*; त्वया *tvayā* = by you; एकाग्रेण *ekāgreṇa* = by single pointed; चेतसा *cetasā* = mind; कच्चित् *kaccit* = whether; अज्ञान-संमोहः *ajñāna-sammohaḥ* = the distraction caused by ignorance; प्रनष्टः *pranaṣṭaḥ* = has been dispelled; ते *te* = your; धनंजय *Dhananjaya* = *O Dhanañjaya.*

72. *Has this been heard, O son of* Pṛthā, *with single pointed mind? Has the distraction, caused by your ignorance,' been dispelled,* O Dhanañjaya.

Here, we find Lord *Kṛṣṇa*, the teacher of the *Gītā*, putting a leading question to his disciple, *Arjuna*, giving him a chance to say how much he has benefited from the discourses. Of course, *Kṛṣṇa* had no doubt about it; but it is only like a doctor, who, confident of his own achieved success, looks at the beaming face of the revived patient and enquries "how are you feeling now?" This is only to enjoy the beaming satisfaction that comes to play on the face of the relieved patient.

'Have you been listening with attentive mind?:- The very question implies that if you have been attentive you must have understood sufficiently the logic in the things, beings and happenings around, and therefore, your relationship with them also. The study of Vedanta broadens our vision, and we start recognising, in a new light, the same old scheme of things around us, and then its previous ugliness gets lifted as thought by magic.

Has your distraction of thought, caused by 'ignorance, been dispelled?':- The false values that we entertain distort our vision of the world and our judgement of its affairs. The delusion of mind was expressed by *Arjuna* in the opening chapters of the *Gītā* (I-36 to 46, and II-4 and 5).

Amputating a septic toe to save the body is no crime; on the contrary it is a life-giving blessing; it is not a toe destroyed, but it is a body and its life saved. The cultural crisis of those times had egged the *Kaurava-s* on to rise up in arms against the beauty of the spiritual culture of the land. *Arjuna* was called upon by the era to champion the cause of the righteous. It was indeed a false reading of the situation that perverted the judgement of the *Pāṇḍava* Prince, as a consequence of which he became utterly broken down, and came to entertain a neurotic condition in himself. The fundamental cause of all confusions was his own "non-apprehension of the Reality," called in *Vedānta* philosophy as "ignorance" (*Ajñāna*). When this "ignorance" is removed by the "Apprehension of the Reality," termed as "knowledge" (*Jñāna*); the entire by-products of "ignornace" are all, in one sweep, eliminated. Hence the logic of this enquiry from the teacher.

True "knowledge" expresses itself in one's own dexterity in action and it should fulfil itself in the splendour of its achievements in the service of society. In case *Arjuna* has understood the philosophy of the *Gītā* he will no more hesitate to meet the challenges as they reach him. This seems to be the unsaid idea in the heart of the Lord.

Arjuna *confesses that his confusions have ended:*

अर्जुन उवाच -
नष्टो मोहः स्मृतिर्लब्धा त्वत्प्रसादान्मयाच्युत ।
स्थितोऽस्मि गतसन्देहः करिष्ये वचनं तव ॥ ७३॥

Arjuna Uvaca-
Naṣṭo mohaḥ smṛtir-labdhā tvat-prasādān-mayā-cyuta,
sthito-' smi gata-sandehaḥ kariṣye vacanaṁ tava.

नष्टः *Naṣṭaḥ* = is desroyed; मोहः *mohaḥ* = delusion; स्मृतिः *smṛtiḥ* = memory (knowledge); लब्धा *labdhā* = has been gained; त्वत् प्रसादात् *tvat-prasādāt* = through your grace; मया *mayā* = by me; अच्युत *acyuta* = *O Acyuta*; स्थित: *sthitaḥ* = firm; अस्मि *asmi* = (I) am; गतसन्देह: *gata-sandehaḥ* = freed from doubts; करिष्ये *kariṣye* = (I) will do; वचनम् *vacanam* = word; तव *tava* = your;

Arjuna said :

73. Destroyed is my delusion, as I have now gained my memory (knowledge) through your grace, O Acyuta. I am firm; my doubts are gone. I will do according to your word (bidding).

Somewhat like one who has suddenly awakended from an unconsicous state, *Arjuna*, with a regained self-recognition, assuredly confesses that his confusions have ended-not because he has unquestioningly swallowed the arguments in the discourses of the *Gītā*, but because, as he himself says "I have gained a *re-cognition* of my Real Nature. The hero in me has now become awakened, and the neurotic condition that had temporarily conquered my mind has totally ended."

Such a revival within and a re-discovery of our personality are possible for all of us only if we truly understand the significance of the *Gītā* philosophy. The Infinite nature of Perfection is our own. It is not something that we have to gain from somewhere by the intervention of some outer agency. This Mighty Being within ourselves is now lying veiled beneath our own ego-centric confusions and abject fears. Even while we are confused and confounded, and helplessly suffering the tragic sorrows of our ego, we are in *reality*, none other than our own Self. When the dream ends, the confusions also end, and we awaken to our Real Nature. So too, in life, this awakening of the Divine in us is the ending of the beast within.

In this new-found equilibrium, born out of Wisdom, experiences as unshakable balance established upon firm foundations and hesitations, fears and weaknesses have left him (*gatasandehaḥ*).

With such a revived personality, when *Arjuna* re-evaluates the situation, he finds no difficulty at all in discovering what exactly his duty is. He openly declares, "I will do according to your word," for in the *Gītā*, Lord *Kṛṣṇa* stands for the Divine-Spark-of-Existence manifested as "pure-intelligence." *Arjuna* here confesses that no more shall he listen to the whisperings of the lower beast in him: the misguiding mind and its agitations.

All students-who have thus fully understood the Gitā, have a clear picture of the goal-of-life, who know what 'path' to follow and how to withdraw from the false by-lanes of existence-will surrender themselves, each to his own integrated inner personality. To surrender ourseves to our own "higher intellect" and to declare confidently and with faith, "*I shall do thy bidding*," is the beginning and the end of all spiritual life.

Sañjaya *glorifies the* Gītācārya *and His Divine Song, the* Gītā*:*

संजय उवाच -

इत्यहं वासुदेवस्य पार्थस्य च महात्मनः।
संवादमिममश्रौषमद्भुतं रोमहर्षणम् ॥७४॥

Sañjaya *Uvaca-*

ityahaṁ vāsudevasya pārthasya ca mahātmanaḥ,
saṁvādam-imam-aśrauṣam-adbhutam roma-harṣaṇam.

इति *iti* = thus; अहम् *aham* = I; वासुदेवस्य *vāsudevasya* = of *Vāsudeva* पार्थस्य *pārthasya* = of *pārtha*; च *ca*-= and; महात्मनः *mahātmanaḥ* = high-souled; संवादम् *saṁvādam* = dialogue; इमम् *imam* = this; अश्रौषम् *aśrauṣam* = (I) have heard; अद्भुतम् *adbhutam* = wonderful; रोमहर्षणम् *roma-harṣaṇam* = which cause the hair to stand on end.

Sañjaya said :

74. *Thus have I heard this wonderful dialogue between* Vāsudeva *and the high-souled* Pārtha, *which causes the hair to stand on end.*

In the previous stanza, when one carefully understands the full significance of the assertion made by the rediscovered, and therefore, revived *Arjuna*, one cannot avoid remembering a parallel declaration made by another teacher of the world, when the revived from his temporary confusion (*Arjuna-sthiti*). When he regained his spiritual balance, which he, as it were, lost temporarily while carrying the cross through the taunting crowd, Jesus also cried: "*Thy will be done.*" Here *Arjuna*, revived by the Grace of *Kṛṣṇa*, similarly cries, "I shall act according to your word (*Kariṣye Vacanam Tava*)." In both cases we find that the statements are almost identical, and while declaring thus, there can be no more any sense of separate existence for the declarer from the Infinite Godhood.

Earlier, at the opening of the *Gītā* , the Pandava Prince said to *Govinda*: "*I shall not fight*," (Ch. II-9) and became despondent; it is the same *Arjuna*, now entirely revived and fully rehabilitated, who declares: "*I shall abide by Thy will.*" The cure is complete and with this the *Śāstra* also ends.

The eighteen-chapter-long *Gītā* is a portion in "*Bhīṣma*-parva" in the *Mahābhārata*. *Vyasa*, the literary artist, has to weave this immortal poem into the warp and woof of the wider canvas of the classic. These closing five stanzas are made use of for this prupose. The beautiful pendant of the *Gītā*, so artistically perfected, is being hooked on to the wondrous necklace of the *Mahābhārata* by these closing five stanzas with which *Sañjaya* concludes his 'running commentary' containing, in very few chosen expressions, the glory of the *Gītā*, the miraculous revival of *Arjuna*, the subjective reaction in *Sañjaya* himself as he listened to this wondrous coversation, and a declaration of Sanjaya's own faith in the true culture of the *Hindūs*.

Thus have I heard this dialogue between Vāsudeva and the high-souled Arjuna:- In the context of the *Vyāsa*-literature, the conversation between *Vāsudeva*, Lord *Kṛṣṇa*, and the son of Pṛthā, *Arjuna*, is but a silent mystic dialogue between the "higher" and the "lower" in man, the "Spirit" and the "Matter." *Vāsudeva* means the Lord (Deva) of the *Vasu-s*; the eight *Vasu-s (Aṣṭa-vasu)* together preside over Time. Therefore, *Vāsudeva*, in its mystic symbolism, stands for the Consciousness that illumines the "concept of Time" projected by the intellect of man. In short, *Vāsudeva* is the Atman, the Self. Pārtha represents matter (earth) which is capable of shedding itself, sheath by sheath* and emerge out as the Pure Eternal Spirit, the Supreme. This act of understanding himself as different from his matter-vestures is man's highest art, the Art of unveiling the Infinite through the finite. The technique of

---

* See the discussion of the five sheaths of *matter (Pañca-kośa)* in *Svāmījī's* Discourses on *Taittirīyopaniṣad;* also read *Svāmījī's* Meditation and life.

this art is the theme of the *Gītā*.

Wonderful (Adbhutam) **:-** This philosophy of the *Gītā*, listened to so far by *Sañjaya*, is reviewed by him as "miraculous" and "wonderful." Every philosophy, no doubt, is a marvel of man's intellect and represents its subtle visions and powers of comprehension. But the philosophy of the *Gītā* was indeed a shade more marvellous and wonderful to *Sañjaya* because, it revived the *blasted* personality of *Arjuna* into a dynamic whole. Because of this practical demonstration of its powers to bless man, the *Gītā* philosophy has acquired the marvellous lustre of the rare shine of the marvellous.

It has proved, beyond all doubt, that every average human being is endowed with potential power with which he can easily conquer all the expressions of life in him and command them to manifest exactly as he wants. He is the Lord of his life, the master of the vehicles, and not a victim of some other mightier power that has created him, only to be endlessly teased by the whims and fancies of this own body, mind and intellect. When this truth is revealed, it is but human for *Sañjaya*, in ecstacy, to exclaim: "Oh! what a marvellous revelation! What a stupendous demonstration!! Adbhutam!!!"

High-souled Pārtha **:-** In the stanza *Arjuna* has been glorified and not Lord *Kṛṣṇa*, the Pārthasārathi. The *Pāṇḍava* Prince, *Arjuna*, had the courage and heroism to come out of his mental confusions, when he gained the right knowledge from his Master's teachings. Certain acts of a child call forth our admiration, but the same acts performed by a grown-up person, look perhaps ridiculous and childish. To the omnipotent Lord, the declaration of the whole *Gītā* itself is but a love play. But, for the confused *Arjuna* to understand the philosophy, and heroically walk out of his confusions is indeed an achievement, worthy of appreciation. Thus Kṛṣṇa, the All perfect, is almost ignored, but *Arjuna*, the mortal, who has understood the art of living as expounded in the Gītā, and has actually revived himself by living it, is heartily congratulated and glorified!

Sañjaya's sympathies were with the *Pāṇḍava-s*; but as an employed minister, he was eating the salt of *Dhṛtarāṣṭra*, and it was not *Dharma* for him to be disloyal to his master. At the same time, in the context of the politics of that time, *Dhṛtarāṣṭra* was, perhaps, the only one who, even then, could stop the war. Diplomatically, *Sañjaya* tries his best, in these stanzas, to bring into the blind man's heart the suggestion of a peace treaty. He makes the blind king understand that Lord *Kṛṣṇa* has revived and re-awakened the hero in *Arjuna*. The blind king is reminded of what the consequences would be: the death and disaster to his hundred children, the pangs of separation in his old age, the dishonour of it all all these are brought home to *Dhṛtarāṣṭra*. But the tottering king's "blindless" seems to be not only physical but also mental and intellectual, for Sanjaya's beseeching moral suggestions fall on the deaf ears of the blind elder.

Sañjaya expresses with open acknowledgement his indebtedness to Śrī Vyāsa Bhagavān:

व्यासप्रसादाच्छ्रुतवानेतद्गुह्यमिदं परम् ।
योगं योगेश्वरात्कृष्णात्साक्षात्कथयतः स्वयम् ।।७५।।

Vyāsa-prasādāc-chrutavān-etad-guhyam-idaṁ param,
yogaṁ yogeśvarāt-kṛṣṇāt-sākṣāt-kathayataḥ svayam.

व्यास-प्रसादात् *vyāsa-prasādāt* = through the grace of *Vyāsa* ; श्रुतवान् *śrutavān* = I have heard; एतत् *etat* = this गुह्यम् *guhyam* = secret; अहम् *aham* = I; परम् *param* = supreme; योगम् *yogam* = Yoga; योगेश्वरात् *yogeśvarāt* = from the Lord of *Yoga*; कृष्णात् *kṛṣṇat* = from *Kṛṣṇa*; साक्षात् *sākṣāt* = directly; कथयतः *kathayataḥ* = declaring; स्वयम् *svayam* = Himself.

75. Through the grace of Vyāsa *I have heard, this supreme and most secret Yoga, directly from* Kṛṣṇa *the Lord of Yoga, Himself declaring it.*

Before the great battle started, *Vyāsa* had approached *Dhṛtarāṣṭra* to offer him the "power of vision" to witness the war; however, the weak-hearted king had not the courage to accept the offer. The king had then suggested that if this power could be given to *Sañjaya*, the king could, through the faithful minister, listen to a running commentary of what was happening on the *Kurukṣetra* battle-field. It was thus from *Vyāsa* that *Sañjaya*, sitting in the carpeted chambers of the Kaurava palace, gained the special faculty of witnessing all that happened and listening to all that was said at the distant battle-field. Grateful to *Śrī Veda Vyās* for having given him this wonderful chance of listening to this "Supreme and most profound *Yoga*," *Sañjaya* is mentally prostrating to the incomparable poet-sage, the author of the *Mahābhārata*.

***Directly from Kṛṣṇa himself* (*Yogeśvarāt Kṛṣṇāt*):-** The suggestion is not that *Sañjaya* had never heard the philosophy of the *Upaniṣad-s* ever before, and that the novelty of the revelation had stunned him; but that his joy is due to the fact that he got a chance to listen to the Eternal Knowledge of the Upaniṣad-s directly from the Lord-of-all-*Yoga-s, Śrī Kṛṣṇa* Himself (*Sākṣāt*) from His own sacred lips.

Here also we can see how Sanjaya is sincerely trying to make the blind *Dhṛtarāṣṭra* realise that it is not *Kṛṣṇa*, the son of *Devakī*, nor the cowherd boy, but it is the Lord Himself, the Yogesvarah who has revived *Arjuna*, and who is serving His devotee as his charioteer. The blind king is reminded that his children, though they have marshalled a large army, stand doomed to destruction, since they have to face the Infinite Lord Himself in their enemy ranks.

The deep impression created by this irresistible philosophy on the devoted heart of Sañjaya is vividly painted:

राजन्संस्मृत्य संस्मृत्य संवादमिममद्भुतम् ।
केशवार्जुनयोः पुण्यं हृष्यामि च मुहुर्मुहुः ।।७६।।

Rājan-saṁsmṛtya saṁsmṛtya
saṁvādam-imam-adbhutaṁ,
keśav-ārjunayoḥ puṇyaṁ
hṛsyāmi ca muḥur-muhuḥ.

राजन् *rājan* = O King; संस्मृत्य *samsmṛtya* = having remembered; संस्मृत्य *samsmṛtya* = having remembered; संवादम् *samvādam* = the dialogue; इमम् *imam* = this; अद्भुतम् *adbhūtam* = wonderful; केशव अर्जुनयोः *keśav-ārjunayoḥ* = between *Keśava* and *Arjuna*; पुण्यम् *puṇyam* = holy; हृष्यामि *hṛsyāmi* = (I) rejoice; च *ca* = and; मुहुः *muhuḥ.* = again; मुहुः *muhuḥ.* = again;

76. *O King! remembering this wonderful and holy dialogue between* Keśava *and* Arjuna, *I rejoice again and again.*

Herein we have a clear statement of *Sañjaya's* reactions to his listening to the Lord's Song. He says, "*this discourse between Kṛṣṇa and Arjuna*"-between God and man, between the Perfect and the imperfect, between the "higher" and the "lower"-is at once "*wonderful and holy.*"

The vision and impression created in his heart by the philosophy that was heard are so deep and striking, that *Sañjaya* admits how irresistibly the memory of those works rises up again and again in his bosom, giving him "the thrill of joy" (*Harṣam*).

Indirectly, Vyāsa is prescribing the method of study of the Gītā. It being "a handbook of instructions" on the Art of Living, it has to be read again and again, repeatedly reflected upon and continuously remembered, until the inner man in us is completely re-educated in the way-of-life that the Gītā charts out for man. The reward for such a painstaking study, and consistency of application has also been clearly pointed out.

One rejoices when one comes to recognise a definite purpose in the otherwise purposeless pilgrimage of man, from the womb to the tomb, called `life.' The study of the Gītā gives not only a purpose to our every-day existence but also a positive message of hope and cheer to the world. The Gītā picks us up from the by-lanes of life and enthrones us as the sovereign power that rules, commands and orders our own life within.

Thus the *Gītā* is an infinite fountain-head of inspiration and joy. It provides our mind with a systematic scheme of re-education whereby it can discover a secret power in itself to tackle intelligently the chaotic happenings around us which constitute our world of challenges. The *Gītā*-educated man learns to recognise a rhythm, to see a beauty, and to hear a melody in the ordinary day-to-day life-a life which was till then but a mad death-dance of appearances and dis-appearances of things and beings.

Sañjaya *confesses that not only the philosophy enchants his minds, but even the memory of the Lord's wondrous form as the total manifested universe has a magic of its own which warms up his heart:*

तच्च संस्मृत्य संस्मृत्य रूपमत्यद्भुतं हरेः ।
विस्मयो मे महान् राजन् हृष्यामि च पुन पुनः ।।७७।।

Tac-ca saṁsmṛtya saṁsmṛtya
rūpam-aty-adbhutaṁ hareḥ,
vismayo me mahān rājan
hṛṣyāmi ca punaḥ punaḥ.

तत् *tat* = that; च *ca* = and; संस्मृत्य *samsmṛtya* = having remembered; संस्मृत्य *saṁsmṛtya* = having remembered; रूपम् *rūpam* = the form; अति अद्भुतम् *ati adbhūtam* = the most wonderful; हरेः *hareḥ* = of *Hari;* विस्मयः *vismayaḥ* = wonder; मे *me* = my; महान् *mahān* = great; राजन् *rājan.* = O king; हृष्यामि *hṛṣyāmi* = (I) rejoice; च *ca* = and; पुनः *punaḥ* = again;

77. Remembering and again remembering, that most wonderful Form of Hari, great is my wonder, O king; and I rejoice again and again.

As I often remember repeatedly that most wonderful form of Hari:- Lord Kṛṣṇa, the charioteer, gave the vision of His Cosmic-Form (*Viśvarūpa*) in an earlier chapter (XI-5 to 47), it is that Form that is indicated by *Sañjaya* here. The Cosmic-Form of the Lord is as impressive to the man-of-heart, as the philosophy of the *Gītā* is unforgettable to the man-of-intelligence. The concept of the Lord's "Total-Form" is staggering in the *Veda-s*, and no doubt, highly impressive in the *Gītā*; but it need not necessarily be a mere poetic vision of the great *Vyāsa*; there are many others whose experiences are almost parallel.*

To a great devotee, remembering the form of the beloved of his heart is itself an ecstatic joy, and where love is, there, in repeated onward gushes, the mind automatically reaches and every time his mind, in that state of love divine, recognises that every existing thing in the world, sentient and insentient, is but His incomparable Infinite form. To such a devotee, heat and cold are He,

---

* In 'Studies in the History and Methods of Science,' edited by Carles Singer (1937), the editor quotes the report of a vision which saint Hildegard (1098-1180) had; she saw 'a fair human form' which declared to her His identity in almost identical words as the description in the *Gītā*: 'I am that Supreme and fiery force that sends forth all the sparks of life. Death hath no part in me, yet do I allot it, wherefore I am girt about with wisdom as with wings. I am that living and fiery essence of the divine substance that glows in the beauty of the field. I shine in the waters, I burn in the sun and the moon and the stars. Mine is that mysterious force of the visible wind. I sustain the the breath of all living. I breathe in the verdure and in the flowers, and when the waters flow like living, it is I. I formed those columns that support the whole earth... all these live because I am in them and am of their life. I am wisdom. Mine is the blast of the thundered word by which all things were made, I permeate all things that they may not die. I am life.'

joys and sorrows are but the play of the Lord; honour and dishonour are but the teasing jokes of the Lover of his heart! Recognising thus, in and through life, everywhere the harmony form, the heart of a true devotee dances in joy at everything, on all occasions.

If the philosophy of the *Gītā*, as it reveals to us the glorious purpose in life, inspires and thrills the thinking aspect in man, the vision of the smiling Lord of *Vṛndāvana* *behind* every name and form, *beneath* every experience, *under* every situation, adds a life-giving joy and a maddening ecstasy to the drunken heart of love.

Given the freedom, I suppose, *Sañjaya* would have written a full length *Sañjaya*-song on the Lord's Divine Song! When the head is thrilled with the silence of understanding and the heart is intoxicated with the embrace of love, man gets transported into a sense of inspired fulfilment.

To express that satisfaction, language is but a frail vehicle; therfore, without dilating much upon what is uppermost in his mind, *Sañjaya* summarises them all into a declaration of his burning faith in this concluding stanza of the Bhagavad Gītā:

यत्र योगेश्वरः कृष्णो यत्र पार्थो धनुर्धरः ।
तत्र श्रीर्विजयो भूतिर्ध्रुवा नीतिर्मतिर्मम ॥७८॥

Yatra Yogeśvaraḥ kṛṣṇo yatra pārtho dhanur-dharaḥ,
tatra śrīr-vijayo bhūtir-dhruvā nītir-matir-mama.

यत्र *yatra* = wherever; योगेश्वरः *yogeśvaraḥ* = the Lord of Yoga; कृष्णः *Kṛṣṇaḥ* = *Kṛṣṇa*; यत्र *yatra* = wherever; पार्थः *pārthaḥ* = *pārtha*; धनुर्धरः *dhanur-dharaḥ* = the archer;

तत्र *tatra* = there; श्रीः *śrīḥ* = prosperity; विजयः *vijayaḥ* = victory; भूतिः *bhūtiḥ* = expansion; ध्रुवा *dhruvā* = sound, firm, steady; नीतिः *nītiḥ* = policy; मतिः *matiḥ* = conviction; मम *mama* = my.

78. *Wherever is* Kṛṣṇa, *the Lord of* Yoga, *wherever is Pārtha, the archer, there are prosperity, victory, happiness and firm (steady or sound) policy; this is my conviction.*

This is the closing stanza of *ŚRĪMAD BHAGAVAD GĪTĀ,* which contains altogether seven hundred and one verses.* This concluding verse has not been sufficiently thought over and commented upon by the majority of commentators of the *Gītā.* The superficial word-meaning of the verse, in fact, can only impress any intelligent student, at its best, as rather drab and dry. After all *Sañjaya* is expressing his private faith in and his personal opinion about something which the readers of *Gītā* need not necessarily accept as final. *Sañjaya,* in effect, says: "Where there is *Kṛṣṇa,* the Lord of *Yoga,* and *Arjuna,* ready with his bow, there prosperity (*Śrī*), success (*Vijaya*), expansion (*Bhūti*), and sound policy (*Dhruva-nīti*) will be: this is my sure faith."

After all, a student of the *Gītā* is not interested in *Sañjaya's* opinion, and it almost amounts to a foul and secret indoctrination, if *Sañjaya* means, diplomatically, to

---

* There are others who consider the *Gītā* as having only 700 stanzas. It is because there is a controversy regarding the opening stanza of the 13th Chapter which contain a question that *Arjuna* asks. This stanza, attributed to Arjuna, is not available in some manuscrips; therefore, without it, the text has only 700 stanzas arranged in its 18 chapters. See our commentary on the opening stanza of chapter 13.

inject into us his own personal opinion. The *Gītā*, as a "Universal Scripture" would have fallen from its own intrinsic dignity as "the Bible of man" had this stanza no Eternal Truth to suggest, which readily invokes a universal appeal. The perfect artist, *Vyāsa*, could never have made such a mistake; indeed, there is a deeper significance in which an unquestionable truth has been expounded.

***Kṛṣṇa the Lord of Yoga* (*Yogeśvaraḥ Kṛṣṇaḥ*) :-** All through the *Gītā*, *Kṛṣṇa* represented the Self, the *Atman*. This spiritual core is the ground upon which the entire play of happenings is staged. He can be invoked within the bosom of each one of us through any one of the *Yoga*-techniques expounded in the *Gītā*.

***Arjuna ready with his bow* (*Pārtho-Dhanurdharaḥ*):** *Pārtha* represents, in this text book, "the confused, limited, ordinary mortal, with all his innumerable weaknesses, agitations and fears." When he has thrown down his "instrument" of effort and achievement, his bow, and has reclined to impotent idleness, no doubt, there is no hope for any success or propserity. But when he is "*ready with his bow*," when he is no more idle but has a willing readiness to use his faculties to brave the challenges of life, there, in that man, we recognise a "*Pārtha ready with his bow*"

Now putting these two pictures together-Lord *Kṛṣṇa* the *Yogeśvaraḥ*, and *Arjuna*, the *Dhanurdharaḥ*- the symbolism of a way-of-life gets completed, wherein, reinforced with spiritual understanding, man gets ready to exert and pour in his endeavours, to tame life and master prosperity. In such a case, there is no power that can stop him from success. In short, the creed of the *Gītā* is that spirituality can be lived in life, and true spiritual understanding is an asset to a man engaged in the battle-of-life.

Today's confusions in society and man's helpless insignificance against the flood of events-inspite of all his achievements in science and mastery over *matter*-are seen, because the *Yogeśvaraḥ* in him is lying neglected, uninvoked. A happy blending of the sacred and the secular is the policy for man as advised in the *Gītā*. In the vision of *Śrī Veda Vyāsa*, he sees a world-order in which man pursues a way-of-life, where in the spiritual and the material production can, no doubt, bring immediately a spectacular flood of wealth into the pockets of man, but not peace and joy into his heart. Prosperity without peace within is a calamity, gruesome and terrible!

The stanza at the same time refuses to accept the other extreme: *Yogeśvara Kṛṣṇa* could have achieved noting on the battle-filed of *Kurukṣetra* without the *Pāṇḍava* Prince, *Arjuna*, "*armed and ready to fight*." Mere spirituality without material exertion and secular achievements will not make life dynamic. I have been trying my best to bring out, as clearly as I can, this running vein of thought throughout the *Gītā*, which expounds the Philosophy of Harmony and explains its plan for man's enduring happiness.

Kṛṣṇa in the *Gītā*, stands for the marriage between the secular and the sacred. Naturally, it is the ardent faith of *Sañjaya** that when a community or nation has its masses galvanized to endure, to act, and to achieve (*Pārtha*, the bowman) and if that generation is conscious of and

---

* *Samjaya--Sam+jaya*, 'the victoriously self-controlled, completely self-mastered.

has sufficiently invoked the spiritual purity of head and heart in themselves (*Kṛṣṇa*, the Lord-of-*Yoga*), in that generation, prosperity, success, expansion, and a sound and sane policy become the natural order.

Even in the arrangement of these terms-prosperity, success, expansion and sound policy-there is an undercurrent of logic which is evident to all students of world history. In the context of modern times and the political experiences, we know that without an *intelligent and steady policy,* no government can lead a nation to any substantial achievement. With a sound policy, *expansion* of all the dormant faculties in the community is brought out, and then only the spirit of co-ordination and brotherhood in the fields of achievement comes to play. In this healthy spirit of love and cooperation, when disciplined people work hard, and when their efforts are intelligently channelised by the sound policies of the government, success cannot be far away. Success thus earned, as a result of national endeavour, disciplined and channelised by a firm, intelligent policy, should necessarily yield true *propserity.* A saner philosophy we cannot find even in modern political thought!!

To make myself more clear:-Enduring prosperity must be that which arises from successful endeavour, that is the result of co-operative and loving effort and this cannot yield any success unless it is nurtured and nourished, guarded and protected, by an intelligent and sound policy.

Thus read, it becomes quite clear that it is not only *Sañjaya's* faith, but it is the ardent conviction of all men of self-control and disciplined mind (*Sañjaya's*), trained to think independently.

There are some commentators of the *Gītā*, who draw our attention to this concluding word in the *Gītā*, "my" (*mama*), and to the opening word in the *Gītā*, "*Dharma*."* Between these two words the seven hundred stanzas are hung together as a garland of immortal beauty, and so these commentators summarize the meaning of the *Gītā* as "*My Dharma* (*Mama Dharma*). The *Gītā* explains the nature of Truth, My Dharma and how the true life starts when these two are in harmony and come to play in one single individual. The ideal nature of all true students of the *Gītā*, therefore, should be a glorious synthesis of both the *spiritual knowledge* expressed in their equipoise and character, and the *dynamic* love expressed through their service to mankind and their readiness to sacrifice.

ॐ तत्सदिति श्रीमद् भगवद् गीतासु उपनिषत्सु
ब्रह्मविद्यायां योगशास्त्रे श्रीकृष्णार्जुन-संवादे
'मोक्षसंन्यास योगो' नाम अष्टादशोऽध्याय: ।

Om tat-sat-iti Śrīmad Bhagavad Gītāsu Upaniṣatsu
brahma-vidyāyāṁ yoga-śāstre Śri Kṛṣṇārjuna-samvāde
'mokṣa-saṁnyāsa yogo' nāma
aṣṭādaśo'dhyāyaḥ,

Thus, in the Upaniṣad-s *of the glorious Bhagavad* Gītā, *in the Science of the Eternal, in the scripture of Yoga, in the dialogue between* Śrī Kṛṣṇa *and* Arjuna, *the eighteenth discourse ends entitled:*

THE YOGA OF LIBERATION THROUGH RENUNCIAITON

---

* Chapter I, Stanza 1 : *Dharma-kṣetre kuru-kṣetre.*

The closing chapter is entitled as Liberation through Renunciation (*Mokṣa-Saṁnyāsa-Yoga*). This term is very closely reminiscent of the *Asparśa-Yoga* of the *Upaniṣad*-s,[1] and the definition of *Yoga* as given by *Kṛṣṇa* Himself in an earlier chapter.[2] To renounce the false values of life in us is at once to rediscover the Divine natue in each one of us which is the essential heritage of man. To discard the beast in us (*Saṁnyāsa*), is the Liberation (*Mokṣa*) of the Divine in us.[3]

OM TAT SAT

MAMA SADGURU TAPOVANA CARṆAYOḤ

"At the Feet Of My Master Tapovanam."

Om Om Om Om Om

---

1. See *Svāmījī's* Discourses on *Māṇḍūkya* and *Kārikā.*
2. Read *Svāmījī's* commentary upon *Duḥkha-saṁyoga-viyogam-yoga-sañjñitam,* Chapter VI, Stanza 23.
3. For a detailed treatment upon the significances of the various forms in the epilogue, please refer the concluding portions in Chapters I, II and III.

THE BHAGAVAD GĪTĀ
CHAPTER XVIII
INDEX TO BEGINNING OF FIRST LINES

śloka-s

अर्जुन उवाच -

संन्यासस्य महाबाहो तत्त्वमिच्छामि वेदितुम् ।
त्यागस्य च हृषीकेश पृथक्केशिनिषूदन ।। १ ।।

श्रीभगवानुवाच -

काम्यानां कर्मणां न्यासं संन्यासं कवयो विदुः ।
सर्वकर्मफलत्यागं प्राहुस्त्यागं विचक्षणाः ।। २ ।।

त्याज्यं दोषवदित्येके कर्म प्राहुर्मनीषिणः ।
यज्ञदानतपःकर्म न त्याज्यमिति चापरे ।। ३ ।।

निश्चयं श्रृणु मे तत्र त्यागे भरतसत्तम ।
त्यागो हि पुरुषव्याघ्र त्रिविधः संप्रकीर्तितः ।। ४ ।।

यज्ञदानतपःकर्म न त्याज्यं कार्यमेव तत् ।
यज्ञो दानं तपश्चैव पावनानि मनीषिणाम् ।। ५ ।।

एतान्यपि तु कर्माणि सङ्गं त्यक्त्वा फलानि च ।
कर्तव्यानीति मे पार्थ निश्चितं मतमुत्तमम् ।। ६ ।।

नियतस्य तु संन्यासः कर्मणो नोपपद्यते ।
मोहात्तस्य परित्यागस्तामसः परिकीर्तितः ।। ७ ।।

दुःखमित्येव यत्कर्म कायक्लेशभयात्त्यजेत् ।
स कृत्वा राजसं त्यागं नैव त्यागफलं लभेत् ।। ८ ।।

कार्यमित्येव यत्कर्म नियतं क्रियतेऽर्जुन ।
सङ्गं त्यक्त्वा फलं चैव स त्यागः सात्त्विको मतः ।। ९ ।।
न द्वेष्ट्यकुशलं कर्म कुशले नानुषज्जते ।
त्यागी सत्त्वसमाविष्टो मेधावी छिन्नसंशयः ।। १० ।।
न हि देहभृता शक्यं त्यक्तुं कर्माण्यशेषतः ।
यस्तु कर्मफलत्यागी स त्यागीत्यभिधीयते ।। ११ ।।
अनिष्टमिष्टं मिश्रं च त्रिविधं कर्मणः फलम् ।
भवत्यत्यागिनां प्रेत्य न तु संन्यासिनां क्वचित् ।। १२ ।।
पञ्चैतानि महाबाहो कारणानि निबोध मे ।
सांख्ये कृतान्ते प्रोक्तानि सिद्धये सर्वकर्मणाम् ।। १३ ।।
अधिष्ठानं तथा कर्ता करणं च पृथग्विधम् ।
विविधाश्च पृथक्चेष्टा दैवं चैवात्र पञ्चमम् ।। १४ ।।
शरीरवाङ्मनोभिर्यत्कर्म प्रारभते नरः ।
न्याय्यं वा विपरीतं वा पञ्चैते तस्य हेतवः ।। १५ ।।
तत्रैवं सति कर्तारमात्मानं केवलं तु यः ।
पश्यत्यकृतबुद्धित्वान्न स पश्यति दुर्मतिः ।। १६ ।।
यस्य नाहंकृतो भावो बुद्धिर्यस्य न लिप्यते ।
हत्वापि स इमाँल्लोकान्न हन्ति न निबध्यते ।। १७ ।।
ज्ञानं ज्ञेयं परिज्ञाता त्रिविधा कर्मचोदना ।
करणं कर्म कर्तेति त्रिविधः कर्मसंग्रहः ।। १८ ।।
ज्ञानं कर्म च कर्ता च त्रिधैव गुणभेदतः ।
प्रोच्यते गुणसंख्याने यथावच्छृणु तान्यपि ।। १९ ।।

सर्वभूतेषु येनैकं भावमव्ययमीक्षते ।
अविभक्तं विभक्तेषु तज्ज्ञानं विद्धि सात्त्विकम् ।। २० ।।
पृथक्त्वेन तु यज्ज्ञानं नानाभावान्पृथग्विधान् ।
वेत्ति सर्वेषु भूतेषु तज्ज्ञानं विद्धि राजसम् ।। २१ ।।
यत्तु कृत्स्नवदेकस्मिन्कार्ये सक्तमहैतुकम् ।
अतत्त्वार्थवदल्पं च तत्तामसमुदाहृतम् ।। २२ ।।
नियतं सङ्गरहितमरागद्वेषत: कृतम् ।
अफलप्रेप्सुना कर्म यत्तत्सात्त्विकमुच्यते ।। २३ ।।
यत्तु कामेप्सुना कर्म साहंकारेण वा पुन: ।
क्रियते बहुलायासं तद्राजसमुदाहृतम् ।। २४ ।।
अनुबन्धं क्षयं हिंसामनवेक्ष्य च पौरुषम् ।
मोहादारभ्यते कर्म यत्तत्तामसमुच्यते ।। २५ ।।
मुक्तसङ्गोऽनहंवादी धृत्युत्साहसमन्वित: ।
सिद्ध्यसिद्ध्योर्निर्विकार: कर्ता सात्त्विक उच्यते ।। २६ ।।
रागी कर्मफलप्रेप्सुर्लुब्धो हिंसात्मकोऽशुचि: ।
हर्षशोकान्वित: कर्ता राजस: परिकीर्तित: ।। २७ ।।
अयुक्त: प्राकृत: स्तब्ध: शठो नैष्कृतिकोऽलस: ।
विषादी दीर्घसूत्री च कर्ता तामस उच्यते ।। २८ ।।
बुद्धेर्भेदं धृतेश्चैव गुणतस्त्रिविधं शृणु ।
प्रोच्यमानमशेषेण पृथक्त्वेन धनंजय ।। २९ ।।
प्रवृत्तिं च निवृत्तिं च कार्याकार्ये भयाभये ।
बन्धं मोक्षं च या वेत्ति बुद्धि: सा पार्थ सात्त्विकी ।। ३० ।।

यया धर्ममधर्मं च कार्यं चाकार्यमेव च ।
अयथावत्प्रजानाति बुद्धिः सा पार्थ राजसी ।। ३१ ।।
अधर्मं धर्मामिति या मन्यते तमसावृता ।
सर्वार्थान्विपरीतांश्च बुद्धिः सा पार्थ तामसी ।। ३२ ।।
धृत्या यया धारयते मनःप्राणेन्द्रियक्रियाः ।
योगेनाव्यभिचारिण्या धृतिः सा पार्थ सात्त्विकी ।। ३३ ।।
यया तु धर्मकामार्थान्धृत्या धारयतेऽर्जुन ।
प्रसङ्गेन फलाकाङ्क्षी धृतिः सा पार्थ राजसी ।। ३४ ।।
यया स्वप्नं भयं शोकं विषादं मदमेव च ।
न विमुञ्चति दुर्मेधा धृतिः सा पार्थ तामसी ।। ३५ ।।
सुखं त्विदानीं त्रिविधं श्रृणु मे भरतर्षभ ।
अभ्यासाद्रमते यत्र दुःखान्तं च निगच्छति ।। ३६ ।।
यत्तदग्रे विषमिव परिणामेऽमृतोपमम् ।
तत्सुखं सात्त्विकं प्रोक्तमात्मबुद्धिप्रसादजम् ।। ३७ ।।
विषयेन्द्रियसंयोगाद्यत्तदग्रेऽमृतोपमम् ।
परिणामे विषमिव तत्सुखं राजसं स्मृतम् ।। ३८ ।।
यदग्रे चानुबन्धे च सुखं मोहनमात्मनः ।
निद्रालस्यप्रमादोत्थं तत्तामसमुदाहृतम् ।। ३९ ।।
न तदस्ति पृथिव्यां वा दिवि देवेषु वा पुनः ।
सत्त्वं प्रकृतिजैर्मुक्तं यदेभिः स्यात्त्रिभिर्गुणैः ।। ४० ।।
ब्राह्मणक्षत्रियविशां शूद्राणां च परंतप ।
कर्माणि प्रविभक्तानि स्वभावप्रभवैर्गुणैः ।। ४१ ।।

शमो दमस्तपः शौचं क्षान्तिरार्जवमेव च ।
ज्ञानं विज्ञानमास्तिक्यं ब्रह्मकर्म स्वभावजम् ।। ४२ ।।
शौर्यं तेजो धृतिर्दाक्ष्यं युद्धे चाप्यपलायनम् ।
दानमीश्वरभावश्च क्षात्रं कर्म स्वभावजम् ।। ४३ ।।
कृषिगौरक्ष्यवाणिज्यं वैश्यकर्म स्वभावजम् ।
परिचर्यात्मकं कर्म शूद्रस्यापि स्वभावजम् ।। ४४ ।।
स्वे स्वे कर्मण्यभिरतः संसिद्धिं लभते नरः ।
स्वकर्मनिरतः सिद्धिं यथा विन्दति तच्छृणु ।। ४५ ।।
यतः प्रवृत्तिर्भूतानां येन सर्वमिदं ततम् ।
स्वकर्मणा तमभ्यर्च्य सिद्धिं विन्दति मानवः ।। ४६ ।।
श्रेयान्स्वधर्मो विगुणः परधर्मात्स्वनुष्ठितात् ।
स्वभावनियतं कर्म कुर्वन्नाप्नोति किल्बिषम् ।। ४७ ।।
सहजं कर्म कौन्तेय सदोषमपि न त्यजेत् ।
सर्वारम्भा हि दोषेण धूमेनाग्निरिवावृताः ।। ४८ ।।
असक्तबुद्धिः सर्वत्र जितात्मा विगतस्पृहः ।
नैष्कर्म्यसिद्धिं परमां संन्यासेनाधिगच्छति ।। ४९ ।।
सिद्धिं प्राप्तो यथा ब्रह्म तथाप्नोति निबोध मे ।
समासेनैव कौन्तेय निष्ठा ज्ञानस्य या परा ।। ५० ।।
बुद्ध्या विशुद्धया युक्तो धृत्यात्मानं नियम्य च ।
शब्दादीन्विषयांस्त्यक्त्वा रागद्वेषौ व्युदस्य च ।। ५१ ।।
विविक्तसेवी लघ्वाशी यतवाक्कायमानसः ।
ध्यानयोगपरो नित्यं वैराग्यं समुपाश्रितः ।। ५२ ।।

अहंकारं बलं दर्पं कामं क्रोधं परिग्रहम् ।
विमुच्य निर्ममः शान्तो ब्रह्मभूयाय कल्पते ।। ५३ ।।
ब्रह्मभूतः प्रसन्नात्मा न शोचति न काङ्क्षति ।
समः सर्वेषु भूतेषु मद्भक्तिं लभते पराम् ।। ५४ ।।
भक्त्या मामभिजानाति यावान्यश्चास्मि तत्त्वतः ।
ततो मां तत्त्वतो ज्ञात्वा विशते तदनन्तरम् ।। ५५ ।।
सर्वकर्माण्यपि सदा कुर्वाणो मद्व्यपाश्रयः ।
मत्प्रसादादवाप्नोति शाश्वतं पदमव्ययम् ।। ५६ ।।
चेतसा सर्वकर्माणि मयि संन्यस्य मत्परः ।
बुद्धियोगमुपाश्रित्य मच्चित्तः सततं भव ।। ५७ ।।
मच्चित्तः सर्वदुर्गाणि मत्प्रसादात्तरिष्यसि ।
अथ चेत्त्वमहंकारान्न श्रोष्यसि विनङ्क्ष्यसि ।। ५८ ।।
यदहंकारमाश्रित्य न योत्स्य इति मन्यसे ।
मिथ्यैष व्यवसायस्ते प्रकृतिस्त्वां नियोक्ष्यति ।। ५९ ।।
स्वभावजेन कौन्तेय निबद्धः स्वेन कर्मणा ।
कर्तुं नेच्छसि यन्मोहात्करिष्यस्यवशोऽपि तत् ।। ६० ।।
ईश्वरः सर्वभूतानां हृद्देशेऽर्जुन तिष्ठति ।
भ्रामयन्सर्वभूतानि यन्त्रारूढानि मायया ।। ६१ ।।
तमेव शरणं गच्छ सर्वभावेन भारत ।
तत्प्रसादात्परां शान्तिं स्थानं प्राप्स्यसि शाश्वतम् ।। ६२ ।।
इति ते ज्ञानमाख्यातं गुह्याद्गुह्यतरं मया ।
विमृश्यैतदशेषेण यथेच्छसि तथा कुरु ।। ६३ ।।

सर्वगुह्यतमं भूयः श्रृणु मे परमं वचः ।
इष्टोऽसि मे दृढमिति ततो वक्ष्यामि ते हितम् ।। ६४ ।।
मन्मना भव मद्भक्तो मद्याजी मां नमस्कुरु ।
मामेवैष्यसि सत्यं ते प्रतिजाने प्रियोऽसि मे ।। ६५ ।।
सर्वधर्मान्परित्यज्य मामेकं शरणं व्रज ।
अहं त्वा सर्वपापेभ्यो मोक्षयिष्यामि मा शुचः ।। ६६ ।।
इदं ते नातपस्काय नाभक्ताय कदाचन ।
न चाशुश्रूषवे वाच्यं न च मां योऽभ्यसूयति ।। ६७ ।।
य इमं परमं गुह्यं मभ्दक्तेष्वभिधास्यति ।
भक्तिं मयि परां कृत्वा मामेवैष्यत्यसंशयः ।। ६८ ।।
न च तस्मान्मनुष्येषु कश्चिन्मे प्रियकृत्तमः ।
भविता न च मे तस्मादन्यः प्रियतरो भुवि ।। ६९ ।।
अध्येष्यते च य इमं धर्म्यं संवादमावयोः ।
ज्ञानयज्ञेन तेनाहमिष्टः स्यामिति मे मतिः ।। ७० ।।
श्रद्धावाननसूयश्च श्रृणुयादपि यो नरः ।
सोऽपि मुक्तः शुभाँल्लोकान्प्राप्नुयात्पुण्यकर्मणाम् ।। ७१ ।।
कच्चिदेतच्छ्रुतं पार्थ त्वयैकाग्रेण चेतसा ।
कच्चिदज्ञानसंमोहः प्रनष्टस्ते धनंजय ।। ७२ ।।

अर्जुन उवाच –
नष्टो मोहः स्मृतिर्लब्धा त्वत्प्रसादान्मयाच्युत ।
स्थितोऽस्मि गतसन्देहः करिष्ये वचनं तव ।। ७३ ।।

संजय उवाच –

इत्यहं वासुदेवस्य पार्थस्य च महात्मनः ।
संवादमिममश्रौषमद्भुतं रोमहर्षणम् ।। ७४ ।।
व्यासप्रसादाच्छ्रुतवानेतद्गुह्यमहं परम् ।
योगं योगेश्वरात्कृष्णात्साक्षात्कथयतः स्वयम् ।। ७५ ।।
राजन्संस्मृत्य संस्मृत्य संवादमिममद्भुतम् ।
केशवार्जुनयोः पुण्यं हृष्यामि च मुहुर्मुहुः ।। ७६ ।।
तच्च संस्मृत्य संस्मृत्य रूपमत्यद्भुतं हरेः ।
विस्मयो मे महान्राजन्हृष्यामि च पुनः पुनः ।।७७ ।।
यत्र योगेश्वरः कृष्णो यत्र पार्थो धनुर्धरः ।
तत्र श्रीर्विजयो भूतिर्ध्रुवा नीतिर्मतिर्मम ।। ७८ ।।

ॐ तत्सदिति श्रीमद्भगवद्गीतासु उपनिषत्सु
ब्रह्मविद्यायां योगशास्त्रे श्रीकृष्णार्जुन-संवादे
'मोक्षसंन्यास योगो' नाम
अष्टादशोऽध्यायः ।।

TRANSLITERATION AND PRONUNCIATION GUIDE

ॐ	oṁ	home	ॐ	oṁ	Rome
अ	a	fun	ट	ṭa	touch
आ	ā	car	ठ	ṭha	ant-hill
इ	i	pin	ड	ḍa	duck
ई	ī	feet	ढ	ḍha	godhood
उ	u	put	ण	ṇa	thunder
ऊ	ū	pool	त	ta	(close to) think
ऋ	ṛ	rig	थ	tha	(close to)pathetic
ॠ	ṝ	(long ṛ)	द	da	(close to) father
ऌ	ḷ	*	ध	dha	(close to)breathe hard
ए	e	play	न	na	numb
ऐ	ai	high	प	pa	purse
ओ	o	over	फ	pha	sapphire
औ	au	cow	ब	ba	but
अं	aṁ	**	भ	bha	abhor
अ:	aḥ	***	म	ma	mother
क	ka	kind	य	ya	young
ख	kha	blockhead	र	ra	run
ग	ga	gate	ल	la	luck
घ	gha	log-hut	व	va	virtue
ङ	ṅa	sing	श	śa	shove
च	ca	chunk	ष	ṣa	bushel
छ	cha	match	स	sa	sir
ज	ja	jug	ह	ha	house
झ	jha	hedgehog	ळ	(Note 1)	(close to) world
ञ	ña	bunch	क्ष	kṣa	worksheet
त्र	tra	three	ज्ञ	jña	*
ऽ	'	unpronounced अ (a)	ऽऽ	"	unpronounced आ (ā)

Note 1 : "l" itself is sometime used.

* No English Equivalent

** Nasalisation of the preceding vowel.

*** Aspiration of preceding vowel